THE ART OF SACRIFICE IN CHESS

Rudolf Spielmann

Translated by
J. DU MONT

Edited and revised by
FRED REINFELD *and*
I.A. HOROWITZ

DOVER PUBLICATIONS, INC.
New York

Published in Canada by General Publishing Company, Ltd., 30 Lesmill Road, Don Mills, Toronto, Ontario.

Published in the United Kingdom by Constable and Company, Ltd., 3 The Lanchesters, 162–164 Fulham Palace Road, London W6 9ER.

Bibliographical Note

This Dover edition, first published in 1995, is an unabridged and unaltered republication of the 1972 printing of the revised edition of the work first published by the David McKay Company, New York, in 1951. *The Art of Sacrifice in Chess* was originally published in German and English editions in 1935.

Library of Congress Cataloging-in-Publication Data

Spielmann, Rudolf.
    [Richtig opfern! English]
    The art of sacrifice in chess / by Rudolf Spielmann ; translated by J. Du Mont ; edited and revised by Fred Reinfeld and I.A. Horowitz.
        p.   cm.
    Originally published: London : G. Bell, 1935.
    Includes index.
    ISBN 0-486-28449-2
    1. Chess—Middle games. I. Reinfeld, Fred, 1910–1964. II. Horowitz, I. A. (Israel Albert), 1907–1973. III. Title.
GV1450.3.S65   1995
794.1′23—dc20
                                        94-24081
                                           CIP

Manufactured in the United States of America
Dover Publications, Inc., 31 East 2nd Street, Mineola, N.Y. 11501

Contents

INTRODUCTION   vii

1. THE VARIOUS TYPES OF SACRIFICES   1

SHAM SACRIFICES   11
Positional Sacrifices   11
EXAMPLE 1: Spielmann-Pirc, Match, 1931   12
EXAMPLE 2: Spielmann-Schlechter, Ostend, 1906   14
EXAMPLE 3: Pirc-Spielmann, Match, 1931   17
Sacrifices for Gain   20
EXAMPLE 4: Bogolyubov-Spielmann, Magdeburg, 1927   21
EXAMPLE 5: Spielmann-Müller, Ebensee, 1933   23
Mating Sacrifices   26
EXAMPLE 6: Spielmann-Hönlinger, Match, 1929   27
EXAMPLE 7: Spielmann-Dr. Tartakover, Marienbad, 1925   31
EXAMPLE 8: Spielmann-Grünfeld, Carlsbad, 1929   34
EXAMPLE 9: Spielmann-L'hermet, Magdeburg, 1927   36

REAL SACRIFICES   40
Sacrifices for Development   41
EXAMPLE 10: Schories-Spielmann, Scheveningen, 1905   42
EXAMPLE 11: Dr. Bernstein-Spielmann, Ostend, 1906   47
Obstructive Sacrifices   50
EXAMPLE 12: Spielmann-Landau, Match, 1933   52
EXAMPLE 13: Spielmann-Hönlinger, Vienna, 1933   56
EXAMPLE 14: Spielmann-Bogolyubov, Match, 1932   59
EXAMPLE 15: Spielmann-Walter, Trentschin-Teplitz,
            1928   64
Preventive (or Anti-castling) Sacrifice   68
EXAMPLE 16: Spielmann-Duras, Scheveningen, 1905   70

EXAMPLE 17: Spielmann-Mieses, Match, 1910   74
EXAMPLE 18: Mieses-Spielmann, Match, 1910   79
EXAMPLE 19: Gereben-Spielmann, Sopron, 1934   84
Line-Clearance Sacrifices   91
EXAMPLE 20: Spielmann-Flamberg, Mannheim, 1914   91
EXAMPLE 21: Spielmann-Eljaschoff, Munich, 1903   95
EXAMPLE 22: Spielmann-Grünfeld, Teplitz-Schönau,
1922   99
Vacating Sacrifices   103
EXAMPLE 23: Spielmann-Janowski, Giuoco Piano,
Carlsbad, 1907   104
EXAMPLE 24: Spielmann-Réti, Abbazia, 1912   108
Deflecting or Decoy Sacrifices   113
EXAMPLE 25: Spielmann-Forgács, Hamburg, 1910   114
(Castled) King's Field Sacrifice   117
EXAMPLE 26: Spielmann-Dekker, Bussum, 1934   119
EXAMPLE 27: Leonhardt-Spielmann, Nuremberg, 1906   125
EXAMPLE 28: Spielmann-Duras, Ostend, 1907   129
EXAMPLE 29: Spielmann-Bogolyubov, Match, 1932   133
EXAMPLE 30: Becker-Spielmann, Vienna, 1926   138
King-Hunt Sacrifices   146
EXAMPLE 31: Rubinstein-Spielmann, San Sebastian, 1912   148
EXAMPLE 32: Spielmann-Rubinstein, Vienna, 1933   154

2. SACRIFICIAL VALUES   162
THE EXCHANGE SACRIFICE   169
EXAMPLE 33: Dr. Treybal-Spielmann, Teplitz-Schönau,
1922   171
EXAMPLE 34: Spielmann-Dr. Tarrasch, Carlsbad, 1923   176
EXAMPLE 35: Spielmann-Dr. Tartakover, Munich, 1909   180
THE QUEEN SACRIFICE   186
EXAMPLE 36: Spielmann-Maroczy, Vienna, 1907   187
EXAMPLE 37: Spielmann-Möller, Gothenburg, 1920   190
EPILOGUE   196
INDEX OF OPENINGS   198

Introduction

THE BEAUTY OF A GAME OF CHESS IS USUALLY APPRAISED, AND with good reason, according to the sacrifices it contains. Sacrifice—a hallowed, heroic concept! Advancing in a chivalrous mood, the individual immolates himself for a noble idea.

Such sacrifice evokes our homage and admiration even where the idea as such does not meet with our full approval. In chess, which we like to view as a counterpart of life, a sacrifice arouses similar feelings in us. On principle we incline to rate a sacrificial game more highly than a positional game. Instinctively we place the moral value above the scientific. We honor Capablanca, but our hearts beat higher when Morphy's name is mentioned. The magic of the sacrifice grips us and we care nothing for the accompanying circumstances—whether Morphy's opponents were weaker than Capablanca's, how Morphy would fare today, how Capablanca would have played in those far-off days. The glowing power of the sacrifice is irresistible: enthusiasm for sacrifice lies in man's nature.

The experts like to disparage the habit of valuing a game according to the amount of material sacrificed. This is understandable to a certain extent, but nonetheless deplorable. The expert is too preoccupied with technique to be able to share the simple-hearted joy of the multitude. He watches the play not from the auditorium but from the stage itself. He is also perhaps a little case-hardened. But the rank-and-file players have preserved fresh and natural feelings: they are delighted now as always with the combinative style.

In spite of this fact—and the related fact that chess books are after all written for the ordinary player—there is no systematic treatise in chess literature dealing with the nature of the sacrifice in all its variety. That is why I have undertaken to deal with this hitherto neglected subject.

My unpretentious book lays no claim to being exhaustive. It is meant to be a guide, not a textbook—which is unsuitable for the subject.

For this reason I have thought it best to preserve a subjective standpoint by using only my own games by way of illustration. I have given much thought to the characteristics of the sacrifice, and as I have myself played many sacrificial games in the thirty years of my career, I have collected a mass of pertinent information, the fruits of which will be found in this volume. May this material be both useful and stimulating to those who are relatively inexperienced.

Finally, I wish to anticipate the possible reproach that I have written this book for the purpose of self-glorification, because I am reputed to be an attacking, combinative player.

This reputation doubtless has its origin in the fact that in former years I frequently adopted gambit openings. It must be said, however, that any fairly successful player has brought off combinations and sacrifices; the perception of such possibilities forms a part of sound play as much as the knowledge of openings and endgames.

If I have drawn on my own games as illustrations, the reason is not that I think they are the best examples, but that, as a matter of course, I am more familiar with them; I am naturally better able to give the reasons underlying my own combinations.

The art of sacrificing correctly cannot be learned to quite the same degree as expertness in the openings; sacrificial play is much more dependent on personal qualities. That is why every great master goes his own particular way in this field; when it comes to sacrificing, there are many artists and many styles, all of them unique.

1. The Various Types of Sacrifices

IN THE DOMAIN OF PROBLEMS THE VARIOUS SACRIFICIAL THEMES
have long since been classified and given their own nomenclature. In practical chess such a classification has never, to my
knowledge, been attempted. A few combinations, such as
"Philidor's legacy," have their own names; but apart from that,
nothing has been done except an occasional loan from the
problemist, such as "self-block," "vacating sacrifice" and the
like. True, problem composers have a much easier task: their
ideas are preconceived and can be executed without any inter-
ference by an opponent! Superfluous pieces are simply eliminated, so that the underlying idea ultimately appears in purest
form permitting clear-cut diagnosis.

It is otherwise in practical chess. Here well-defined combinations and sacrifices turn up more or less at hazard. Hardly ever
are they "pure" and "economical" as in problems, and consequently they are harder to recognize and classify. This is doubtless one of the reasons why such classification has not yet been
attempted.

I can well imagine that some other author would classify
the various types of sacrifices in an altogether different manner.
That is why I again emphasize my purely subjective point of
view. A definitive treatment cannot be expected from a first
attempt. It will probably take a long time to establish for
practical chess the kind of universally acceptable nomenclature
that exists in the realm of problems.

Sacrifices represent in chess an exceptionally important
phase of the struggle. Beauty is not the sole object. They have

the common aim of increasing the effectiveness of other pieces outside of the normal routine, if possible suddenly. In equalized positions their purpose is to gain time. But mostly they serve to increase already existing advantages and they are consequently particularly adapted to the exploitation of mistakes by the other side. It may be that an advantage in development is turned into a grand assault, or that a weak point in the enemy lines is ripped open in the same way.

The advantage to be exploited need not be of a general nature; it can be merely local. Particularly in such cases does the sacrifice provide an indispensable weapon; for placid play is apt to dissipate the advantage, with resultant drifting into a drawn position.

A sacrifice at the right moment takes opportunity by the forelock. The opponent may gain material, but he is tempted or forced to make some temporarily useless moves, his troops become disordered and the disconnected forces are beaten before they can put up a united front to the enemy.

To get the unwieldy mass of possible sacrifices into some sort of order, we must first classify them under three heads: form, size and object.

Under the heading "form," there are two types: active and passive.

In distinguishing between these two types, the deciding factor, from a scientific point of view, would be whether the sacrifice arises from a move made for the purpose of sacrificing, or from a raid by the enemy. In other words, through moving and offering a piece—or through disregarding the enemy's threat to capture. Thus after 1 P-K4, P-K4; 2 P-KB4 is an active sacrifice. Conversely, after 1 P-K4, P-K4; 2 N-KB3, N-QB3; 3 P-Q4, PxP; 4 NxP, the raid 4 . . . Q-R5 allows the passive sacrifice 5 N-N5.

From a practical point of view, however, I prefer to make

a different distinction, namely, whether or not acceptance of the proffered sacrifice is compulsory. Those which must be accepted I call active, the others passive.

In the Allgaier Gambit (1 P-K4, P-K4; 2 P-KB4, PxP; 3 N-KB3, P-KN4; 4 P-KR4, P-N5; 5 N-N5, P-KR3; 6 NxP) both forms occur in the first six moves. 5 N-N5 is a passive sacrifice, as it can be declined by 5 . . . N-KB3 with no worsening of Black's position. Contrariwise, 6 NxP is an active sacrifice because it has to be accepted.

In the nature of things the active sacrifice is by far the more powerful of the two.

The size of the sacrifice appears to be perfectly easy to determine. But, as we shall see later on, this aspect also presents problems, as the value of each unit varies qualitatively according to the nature of a given position.

There are sacrifices of Pawns and of pieces. The latter can be subdivided into full- and part-sacrifices, depending on whether a whole piece is given up or whether there is partial compensation.

When considering part-sacrifices, we must distinguish between the major and minor pieces. When minor pieces are sacrificed, any material compensation can consist only in Pawns. In the case of a major piece, the compensation may be minor pieces or Pawns or both. The possible resulting situations are quite dissimilar, for after full sacrifices the number of your own units diminishes, while after a part-sacrifice it frequently actually increases.

A separate chapter treats of the sacrifice of the exchange and all its ramifications.

The most important classification of sacrifices is according to their object.

In this respect we must first distinguish between two groups, namely *sham* and *real* sacrifices. The difference is this: sham sacrifices involve losses of material only for a *definable* amount of time; in the case of real sacrifices, the amount of time required for recovering the material is not clear.

Therefore a sham (temporary) sacrifice involves no risk. After a series of forced moves, the player either recovers the invested material with advantage, or else even mates his opponent. The consequences of the sacrifice were foreseen from the first. Properly speaking, there is no sacrifice, only an advantageous business deal.

Yet such sacrifices must not be disparaged; often fine perception and a great deal of imagination are required, as well as the gift of intricate calculation, in order to discern possibilities in a position and exploit them.

We shall divide sham sacrifices into three groups:
1. positional sacrifices
2. sacrifices for gain
3. mating sacrifices

Positional sacrifices lead to forced recovery of the material lost with an improvement in position.

Thus, after 1 P-K4, P-K4; 2 N-KB3, N-QB3; 3 N-B3, B-B4 White can sacrifice advantageously with 4 NxP, for after 4 . . . NxN he recovers the piece by 5 P-Q4, with improved prospects.

The *sacrifice for gain* leads to an advantage in material, the sacrificed material being regained by force and with interest.

An example: 1 P-K4, P-K4; 2 N-KB3, N-QB3; 3 B-N5, P-QR3; 4 B-R4, N-B3; 5 O-O, B-K2; 6 P-Q4, P-QN4; 7 B-N3, NxQP?; 8 BxPch, KxB; 9 NxPch followed by 10 QxN.

The *mating sacrifice* leads to checkmate or, alternatively, to immediately decisive gain of material. The actual mate can frequently be delayed by the heaviest counter-sacrifices (loss of the Queen, for example), which are, in effect, tantamount to mate.

For example: 1 P-K4, P-K4; 2 N-KB3, P-Q3; 3 B-B4, P-KR3; 4 N-B3, N-QB3; 5 P-Q4, B-N5; 6 PxP, NxP?; 7 NxN! If Black now captures the Queen, mate follows by 8 BxPch, K-K2; 9 N-Q5 mate. True, Black can avoid this mate in various ways by declining the sham sacrifice. But in that case White remains a piece to the good.

In real sacrifices the player gives up material, but is unable to calculate the consequences with accuracy; he has to rely on his judgment. He obtains dynamic advantages, which he can realize gradually. Should he not succeed in this, he will most probably lose the game through deficiency in material. Therein lies the risk, and risk is the hallmark of the real sacrifice. This group will occupy most of our attention from now on.

Compared with sham sacrifices, the real sacrifices are much more difficult to treat scientifically. Their secrets reveal themselves only to the gifted and courageous player, who has strong if controlled self-confidence. The timid player will take to real sacrifices only with difficulty, principally because the risk involved makes him uneasy.

The theory of real sacrifices cannot go beyond general rules, advice, warnings and illustrations. But let no one be discouraged: the moderately gifted player can obtain a considerable playing strength by applying himself diligently; while, on the other hand, weak play does not necessarily indicate lack of talent!

Unlike the sham sacrifice, in which the aims are clear as day, the real sacrifice has vaguely defined goals; the result lies in the lap of the gods and at most can be formulated only intuitively.

It follows that it must be a matter of some difficulty to differentiate between the various types of real sacrifices. I have had to adopt a subjective point of view again and to proceed at times by instinct. This conforms, after all, with the nature of these sacrifices, which in actual play are generally decided upon on an instinctive basis.

I have arrived at the following subdivisions:

1. sacrifices for development
2. obstructive sacrifices
3. preventive (or anti-castling) sacrifices
4. line-clearance sacrifices
5. vacating sacrifices
6. deflecting or decoy sacrifices
7. (castled) King's Field sacrifices
8. King-Hunt sacrifices

The *sacrifice for development* aims at an unusual acceleration of one's development. To this type belong more or less all gambits, as, for example the Muzio Gambit (1 P-K4, P-K4; 2 P-KB4, PxP; 3 N-KB3, P-KN4; 4 B-B4, P-N5; 5 O-O, PxN).

The rapid formation of a center which is said by many to be the object of most gambits, is, strictly speaking, only a means to the attainment of that object (accelerated development). In the nature of things the developing sacrifice occurs in the opening stages—when the development on either side is as yet uncompleted.

Besides the developing sacrifices known to theory, new ones are constantly evolved in practical play. For the most part they are Pawn sacrifices, but—as in the Muzio, mentioned above—pieces are sometimes sacrificed as well.

The *obstructive sacrifice* also occurs before the respective developments are completed, and the object is likewise a net plus in development. But here we achieve our objective not by speeding up our own, but by slowing down the opponent's, development. The material staked will have to be of a modest nature. An instance from the Caro-Kann Defense: 1 P-K4, P-QB3; 2 P-Q4, P-Q4; 3 P-K5, B-B4; 4 P-KN4, B-N3; 5 P-KR4, P-KR3; 6 P-K6. [*This last move obstructs the future development of Black's King Bishop.*]

The *preventive* (*anti-castling*) *sacrifice* is intended to prevent the opponent's castling.

To this end even a whole piece can be given up in certain circumstances, namely when it is possible to hold the hostile King in the middle and to open up the center files. In his second match with Lasker, Steinitz gave up a piece early in the game for this purpose:

1 P-K4, P-K4; 2 N-KB3, N-QB3; 3 B-B4, B-B4; 4 P-B3, N-B3; 5 P-Q4, PxP; 6 PxP, B-N5ch; 7 N-B3, NxKP; 8 O-O, BxN; 9 PxB, P-Q4; 10 B-R3.

The *line-clearance sacrifice* aims at the early employment of the Rooks on open lines. The Alekhine variation of the French Defense belongs to this category: 1 P-K4, P-K3; 2 P-Q4, P-Q4; 3 N-QB3, N-KB3; 4 B-N5, B-K2; 5 P-K5, KN-Q2; 6 P-KR4.

After 6 . . . BxB; 7 PxB, QxP White's open King Rook file becomes very powerful. In certain cases this type of sacrifice justifies a very large stake.

The *vacating sacrifice* procures access for a particular unit to a more favorable square. For so limited an object, only a small investment should be risked. A pretty case in point is the following example from the Two Knights' Defense:

1 P-K4, P-K4; 2 N-KB3, N-QB3; 3 B-B4, N-B3; 4 N-N5, P-Q4; 5 PxP, N-QR4; 6 P-Q3, P-KR3; 7 N-KB3, P-K5; 8 Q-K2, NxB; 9 PxN, B-QB4; 10 P-KR3, O-O; 11 N-R2.

Now Black has only one really promising continuation of the attack: 11 . . . P-K6!; 12 BxP, BxB; 13 PxB, N-K5. Thanks to this Knight's strong position, Black's attack is very powerful.

The *deflecting or decoy sacrifice* has the definite object of luring or diverting one or more enemy pieces from the main field of battle. The attacker, for instance, allows his opponent to graze on one wing in order to be able to pursue his attack undisturbed on the other side. Such sacrifices ordinarily occur only after development is far advanced. An example from the Ruy Lopez:

1	P-K4	P-K4	9	P-B3	B-K2
2	N-KB3	N-QB3	10	B-K3	O-O
3	B-N5	P-QR3	11	QN-Q2	N-R4
4	B-R4	N-B3	12	B-B2	NxN
5	O-O	NxP	13	QxN	N-B5
6	P-Q4	P-QN4	14	Q-Q3	P-N3
7	B-N3	P-Q4	15	B-R6	NxNP
8	PxP	B-K3	16	Q-K3	R-K1
			17	Q-B4	....

White has a strong attack against the hostile castled position. Black's Knight is out of play and for the time being is unable to participate in the defense.

Sacrifices in the King's Field have the object of breaking up the hostile King's castled position. They are the most frequent combinations in the middle game and occur in countless variations. They are seldom encountered in the opening stage, requiring as they do an advanced stage of development.

King-Hunt sacrifices I call those which drive the King into the open, where he is automatically exposed to a great many dangers. An example from the Vienna: 1 P-K4, P-K4; 2 N-QB3, B-B4; 3 N-R4, BxPch.

White hardly has an alternative to capturing and must at least attempt to hold the extra piece. But his King will be driven from pillar to post after 4 K×B, Q-R5ch; 5 K-K3, Q-B5ch; 6 K-Q3, P-Q4.

In comparing the two broad groups of sacrifices, we now perceive the train of thought on which this division is based. In the *sham* sacrifice the *ultimate* object is paramount. In the *real* sacrifice, only the *provisional* aim is considered. The common ground in both types is that only the object visible at the time of the sacrifice is taken as the characteristic feature.

In practical play, combinations frequently occur which are composed of several sacrifices. These usually belong to only one of the two main groups. But it is quite possible for a sham sacrifice to precede a real one. The converse can happen in the course of a game, but hardly as part of one combination.

In the following pages, the various types of sacrifices will be treated according to their object, that is, according to their type. Only in two cases will the classification be according to the amount of material given up. These are the sacrifice of the exchange and the Queen sacrifice. The reasons for this are set forth in the respective chapters.

SHAM SACRIFICES

A surprisingly large number of sacrificial combinations must be classed as sham sacrifices, because they lack the real characteristics of the sacrifice.

The material given up is regained subsequently, frequently with interest. They are sham sacrifices in the most literal sense of the word. With these we shall deal in the next three sections.

POSITIONAL SACRIFICES

To this class belong all sacrifices which have the object of effecting an improvement in position by temporarily giving up material. The recapture of the material given up, is an essential characteristic. It is not necessary for the compensation to be in the same currency. But the *quid pro quo*, in the material sense, must be adequate. In effect the positional sacrifice is a form of barter—only the return is not made immediately, but rather in the course of several moves. Again, a positional sacrifice need not necessarily lead to an *advantage* in position. Undertaken in a bad position, it may barely save the game or merely prolong resistance.

However, if when all is said and done the positional sacrifice is only an exchange, it is nevertheless an exceedingly valuable weapon. Of course, one must gauge accurately the consequences of such a deal. This should not be difficult as a rule.

EXAMPLE 1

Queen's Gambit Declined
Match, 1931

WHITE	BLACK	WHITE	BLACK
R. Spielmann	V. Pirc	R. Spielmann	V. Pirc
1 P-Q4	P-Q4	5 P-QR4	B-B4
2 P-QB4	P-QB3	6 P-K3	N-R3
3 N-KB3	N-B3	7 BxP	N-QN5
4 N-B3	PxP	8 O-O	P-K3
		9 Q-K2	N-K5?

Black seeks mechanically to prevent the annoying advance
P-K4, but is all the sooner at a disadvantage.

10 N-K5   B-Q3

In this position Black threatens to free his game by 11 . . .
BxN; 12 PxB, NxN; 13 PxN, B-Q6; but in consequence of
the unhappy move 9 . . . N-K5? his minor pieces are quite
insecure. This circumstance gives White an opportunity for
a decisive positional sacrifice.

11 NxKBP!   . . . .

Not really a sacrifice at all, as White is bound to obtain adequate material compensation. But the important point is that
Black's game becomes disorganized beyond hope of salvation.

<pre>
11 ....   KxN
</pre>

An alternative variation also characterized by a temporary sacrifice is 11 . . . BxPch; 12 KxB, Q-R5ch; 13 K-N1, B-N5; 14 NxN, BxQ; 15 N/B7-Q6ch followed by 16 BxB—when Black has won the Queen but still stands to lose! It is true that White has only three minor pieces for the Queen, which in ordinary circumstances assures equality; but here, considering the exposed position of the Black King, White should quickly obtain a winning attack.

The relative value of the pieces, a vital criterion in appraising this type of sacrifice, is shown here in the most instructive light.

<pre>
12 Q-B3   ....
</pre>

The essential point of the combination. The Knight and Bishop are both attacked and one of them, the Bishop, threatens to be captured with check. Thus Black must willy-nilly give back the piece.

<pre>
12 ....   P-KN3   14 KxB   Q-R5ch
13 NxN   BxPch   15 K-N1   QxN
</pre>

And so Black has even regained his Pawn. But now White's attack against Black's shattered position begins with decisive effect. That is the positional point of the sacrifice. [*Hence White naturally avoids exchange of Queens.*]

| 16 | Q-N3 | KR-K1 | 17 | B-Q2 | Q-B7 |

[If 17 . . . N-B7 or . . . N-Q6 White wins the Queen with 18 P-B3.]

| 18 | B-B3 | N-Q4 | 19 | KR-B1 | Q-K5 |
| | | | 20 | B-Q2 | . . . . |

[Black is helpless against the coming P-B3.]

20	. . . .	P-KN4	23	P-K4	B-N3
21	P-B3	Q-R5	24	PxN	KPxP
22	QxQ	PxQ	25	B-B1	Resigns

EXAMPLE 2

King's Gambit Declined
(in effect)
Ostend, 1906

WHITE	BLACK	WHITE	BLACK
R. Spielmann	C. Schlechter	R. Spielmann	C. Schlechter
1 P-K4	P-K4	6 N-B3	B-KN5
2 B-B4	N-KB3	7 N-QR4	PxP
3 P-Q3	B-B4	8 NxB	PxN
4 N-QB3	P-Q3	9 BxP	N-KR4
5 P-B4	N-B3	10 B-K3	O-O

[So that if 11 BxP, N-K4!; 12 BxR, BxN; 13 PxB, Q-R5ch; 14 K-Q2, RxB with a powerful attack.]

| 11 | O-O! | N-K4 |

The disposition of forces indicates that Black has been striving for the initiative. For this reason he rejects the solid 11 . . . N-Q5 which probably results in quick equality after 12 BxN, PxB; 13 P-KR3, B-K3! Such an ambition on the part of the second player is generally open to question and not infrequently gives rise to surprising turns.

12 NxN!   ....

Probably Black reckoned only on 12 B×P, when 12 . . .
BxN; 13 PxB, NxB; 14 BxR, N-K6 gives Black a winning attack. The text move turns the tables.

12 ....   BxQ   13 NxP   RxN?

An attempt to refute the combination. Correct is 13 . . .
Q-K2 when White's best course is to take a draw by perpetual
check: 14 N-K5 dis ch, K-R1; 15 N-B7ch, K-N1; 16 N-K5 dis
ch etc.

14 BxRch   ....

Very strong also was 14 RxR, K-R1; 15 RxB, P-QN3 (if
15 . . . Q-Q3; 16 R-B5); 16 P-K5 etc. *[This line is definitely
more forcing than Spielmann's continuation.]*

14 ....   K-R1   15 QRxB   N-B3
                          16 BxP   ....

If White, in this position, can preserve his two Bishops, he
will have an easy win with Rook, Bishop and two Pawns for
the Queen. He must however submit to the exchange of one
of the Bishops whereby the position is nearly equalized (see
Part 2, The Queen Sacrifice), although the passed Pawn offers winning chances.

16	P-QN3	17 B-B2	N-N5

| | 18 B-Q5 | .... | |

[Spielmann failed to realize, either during the game or in his annotations, that 18 P-B3!—preventing the subsequent . . . Q-Q5-K6—makes it possible to set the powerful Pawn mass in motion.]

| | 18 .... | P-B3! | |

[For if 19 BxBP?, Q-Q3!—or 19 . . . Q-B2!—wins the Bishop.]

19	B-K6	NxB	23	R-B3	Q-R3
20	RxN	Q-Q5	24	P-KR3	R-K1
21	P-B3	Q-K6	25	B-Q7	R-KB1
22	K-B1	P-N3	26	B-N4	K-N2
			27	P-Q4	....

[27 K-K2, preventing the new inroad of Black's Queen, still offers winning chances.]

27	....	Q-K6	29	B-B3	K-K2
28	RxR	KxR	30	P-K5	K-Q2
				Drawn	

EXAMPLE 3

Dutch Defense
Match, 1931

WHITE	BLACK	WHITE	BLACK
V. Pirc	R. Spielmann	V. Pirc	R. Spielmann
1 P-Q4	P-K3	4 P-KN3	B-N5ch
2 P-QB4	P-KB4	5 B-Q2	BxBch
3 N-KB3	N-KB3	6 QNxB	N-B3

[The exchange has freed Black's game appreciably.]

7 B-N2	O-O	14 N-Q4	NxN
8 O-O	P-Q3	15 QxN	P-B4
9 Q-N3	K-R1	16 Q-B3	B-Q2
10 Q-B3	P-K4!	17 N-B1	B-B3
11 PxP	PxP	18 N-K3	N-Q2
12 QR-Q1	Q-K2	19 B-R3	Q-N4
13 KR-K1	P-K5	20 R-Q6?	....

P-B4 was necessary. *[Black has the makings of a powerful King-side attack.]*

20	Q-R4	22 N-Q5	N-K4
21 K-N2	QR-K1	23 N-B4	Q-B2
		24 N-Q5	....

In this position Black has the better game: his pieces co-operate effectively, while White's forces are in part ineffective, in part even in jeopardy. Black's advantage lies solely in effective development and is therefore evanescent. Hence it is a question of exploiting the advantage before White consolidates his position. A complicated positional sacrifice solves the problem.

24   ....   P-B5!   25 NxP   ....

It is clear that declining the offer entails a serious disadvantage. But acceptance by 25 PxP? loses at once: 25 . . . N-N3; 26 P-K3 (the threat was . . . NxPch, preceded perhaps by . . . BxN), N-R5ch; 27 K-R1 (or 27 K-N3, N-B6; 28 R-QB1, Q-R4 and Black's attack must obviously prevail; he threatens above all . . . Q-R5ch followed by . . . N-N4), N-B6; 28 R-KB1, Q-R4; 29 K-N2, N-R5ch; 30 K-N1, Q-B6 and wins.

25   ....   P-KN4   26 B-K6   ....

Falling in with the combination proper. After 26 N-Q5, QxPch; 27 K-R1, Q-Q5! Black obtains a clearly superior endgame, for example 28 P-N3, BxN; 29 QxQ, PxQ; 30 RxB, P-Q6; 31 PxP, NxQP—or 31 B-N2, N-N5! etc.

26   ....   Q-B3   27 N-R5   ....

27 N-Q5 is answered in the same way.

27   ....   QxPch   28 K-R1   ....

Seemingly White stands to win. How is the terrible threat of 29 QxNch to be parried?

28   ....   R-B3!

The key to the combination initiated by 24 . . . P-B5! Now 25 QxN? fails on account of mate in two. [*Thus White's pin on the Knight is nullified.*]

29 B-Q7? . . . .

A regrettable error which spells immediate downfall.

Correct was 29 NxR, QxN; 30 RxB! (else White loses his Bishop), PxR; 31 B-R3 on which Black intended 31 . . . Q-B7! Now White can hardly prevent the inroad of Black's Queen to Q5. His Rook, entrusted with guarding the King Pawn, can at most move to KB1 with the intention of replying to 32 . . . QxP with 33 R-B8ch. But Black need not capture the Pawn. The logical reply to 32 R-KB1 is 32 . . . Q-Q5. If instead 32 P-K3, K-N1!; 33 R-KB1, Q-K7 with the overpowering threat of 34 . . . N-B6.

Thus Black's Queen will arrive on Q5 after all, maintaining a commanding position there as White cannot afford to exchange Queens. In this way Black gains an advantage which differs in essence from that obtaining before the combination: it no longer rests on development but on positional considerations and is therefore of a durable character.

It is not part of our task to determine whether the advantage thus gained suffices to win. A positional sacrifice is expected to ensure an improvement in position rather than an immediate win. Frequently only slight results are obtained from great exertions. But we are studying a type of sacrifice, not its effect.

29 . . . . RxR 30 BxR R-Q5!
Resigns

Black's last move, as strong as it is obvious, is immediately decisive. The threats . . . BxB or . . . N-N5 cannot both be met.

These three examples will suffice to explain the character of the positional sacrifice.

Essential for the employment of this weapon is a practiced eye for the relative value of the pieces and the knowledge derived from experience. It is necessary to know when the Bishops are better and when the Knights, and how to appraise Pawn formations, etc. On this subject the chapter on values in sacrifices will give useful and varied information.

SACRIFICES FOR GAIN

So we are to sacrifice *in order to achieve material gain!* This appears to be a contradiction in terms, which disappears only when we realize that we are dealing with a sham sacrifice.

As a rule, the opportunity for such combinations arises in already superior positions, sometimes also after serious errors or sins of omission on the opponent's part.

Subjectively, the essentials are sound judgment as to the state of development at the time and a practiced eye for the strength or weakness of a position. Inexperienced or over-optimistic players often neglect their development. They rack their brains over some sham sacrifice which promises them a gain in material, and as often as not commit themselves to it without taking into account the fact that the combination cannot possibly be sound, owing to the state of development. The consequences are painful and often fatal surprises.

Superior development, simultaneous attacks on points which can only be protected with difficulty, loose or badly protected hostile units, finally any kind of weakness in the enemy camp—those are the crucial points where opportunities for temporary

sacrifices can be looked for and where they are frequently
found.

EXAMPLE 4

Caro-Kann Defense
Magdeburg, 1927

| WHITE | BLACK | WHITE | BLACK |
E. Bogolyubov	R. Spielmann	E. Bogolyubov	R. Spielmann
1 P-K4	P-QB3	4 P-K5	N-K5
2 N-QB3	P-Q4	5 P-Q4	B-B4
3 N-B3	N-B3	6 N-KR4	....

Neglecting his development.

6	P-K3	8 NxN	BPxN
7 NxB	PxN	9 Q-N4	Q-Q2
		10 Q-N3	....

The exchange of Queens is better.

| 10 .... | P-QB4 | 11 PxP | N-B3 |
| | | 12 P-QB3 | BxP |

A sacrifice for development. After 13 QxP, O-O-O Black
obviously has much the better of it.

| 13 | B-KB4 | O-O | 15 | PxP e.p. | RxP |
| 14 | B-K2 | P-B4 | 16 | B-K3 | .... |

[Likewise after 16 O-O, QR-KB1; 17 B-K3, R-N3 Black gets a sharp attack.]

| 16 | .... | P-Q5! | 17 | PxP | NxP |
| | | | 18 | BxN | .... |

[The plausible alternative 18 B-B4ch is met by 18 . . . K-R1; 19 O-O, P-QN4!; 20 BxN, QxB; 21 BxP, QxP threatening . . . QxB and also . . . BxPch!]

18	....	QxB	21	QR-K1	QR-KB1
19	O-O	QxP	22	R-K2	Q-Q5
20	B-B4ch	K-R1	23	B-N3	....

The attacker (Black) has by far the better game, principally from the positional point of view. The extra Pawn in itself is not a deciding factor, as there are Bishops on opposite colors. But the pressure on White's KB2 allows a decisive blow to be struck, as his King lacks a loophole. The combination is obvious and arises naturally out of the position.

| 23 | .... | RxP! | 24 | R/K2xR | .... |

If 24 R/B1xR, Q-R8ch and mate in two more moves.

24 ....   RxR   25 QxR   ....

White has to take the Rook; but 25 RxR will not do because
of . . . Q-R8ch leading to mate.

25 ....   Q-K4

The point: Black wins the Queen; and with Queen and two
Pawns against Rook and Bishop he has an overwhelming ad-
vantage. The sham sacrifice has paid off handsomely.
The rest is easy to understand.

26	P-N3	P-KR4	35	K-Q4	K-R3
27	R-Q1	BxQch	36	B-Q5	Q-Q7ch
28	KxB	Q-B3ch	37	K-K4	P-QN4
29	K-K3	Q-KB6ch	38	R-Q3	Q-K7ch
30	K-Q4	P-K6	39	R-K3	Q-B7ch
31	R-Q3	Q-B7	40	K-K5	P-R4
32	RxP	QxKRP	41	K-Q6	P-N3
33	K-K4	Q-N7ch	42	P-N4	PxP
34	K-Q3	K-R2	43	R-K6	P-N5
				Resigns	

EXAMPLE 5

Queen's Gambit Declined
Ebensee, 1933

WHITE	BLACK	WHITE	BLACK
R. Spielmann	H. Müller	R. Spielmann	H. Müller
1 P-Q4	P-Q4	5 P-K3	QN-Q2
2 N-KB3	N-KB3	6 N-K5	B-K2
3 P-B4	P-B3	7 B-Q3	O-O
4 N-B3	P-K3	8 P-B4	P-B4
		9 O-O	Q-B2

[Too slow. 9 . . . Q-N3! was indicated.]

10	BPxP	KPxP	12	PxP	Q-N3
11	Q-B3	PxP	13	B-K3	....

A sacrifice for development.

13	....	QxNP	14	KR-B1	Q-R6
			15	QR-N1	B-Q1?

15 . . . P-QR3 is correct.

16	B-KB2	Q-Q3	17	N-N5	Q-N1
			18	B-N3!	....

Threatening 19 NxN, BxN; 20 P-B5. The bad position of the hostile Queen gives White an early opportunity for a sacrifice for gain.

18	....	N-K5	19	BxN	PxB

20 Q-N3!   . . . .

Much stronger than 20 QxP, N-B3; 21 Q-Q3, P-KN3, when Black still has prospects of relief. The text move is only preliminary to a sacrificial combination which Black cannot prevent.

This frequently happens when the weakness in the defender's camp is of a positional nature, that is, based on the Pawn formation (positional weakness). When the weakness lies in development (dynamic weakness), however, it is only temporary; and if it is to be exploited by means of a sacrifice, there is usually no time for preparation. There are however exceptions, as for instance when the development is particularly backward and when this defect can only be remedied by involved maneuvers. Such a case obtains here. The heaviest fighting piece, the Queen, is not only out of play, but is menaced without having a flight square.

This example shows how harmful such defects in development can be.

After White's last move, he has several powerful threats, such as 21 NxN, BxN; 22 P-B5—or 21 NxBP, RxN; 22 RxB, QxR; 23 N-Q6. These are based on the Black Queen's unhappy lodgment and cannot both be warded off. There follows a short and decisive battle which is easy to understand.

20 . . . .   B-N3

[If 20 . . . NxN; 21 BPxN and Black is helpless against the coming P-K6!]

| 21 | NxBP! | RxN | 23 | K-R1! | BxP |
| 22 | P-B5 | N-K4 | 24 | BxN | Q-K1 |

He cannot save the exchange. Other moves would lead to the same continuation.

| 25 | N-Q6 | Q-K3 | 27 | RxQ | KxN |
| 26 | NxR | QxQ | 28 | R-B1 | K-K3 |

Forced; if 28 . . . K-N3?; 29 R-N3ch.

29	BxP	R-KN1	35	P-R5	BxRP
30	B-K5	R-Q1	36	R-B5	B-N5
31	R-N5	B-N3	37	B-B6ch	K-K3
32	P-KR4	B-K1	38	BxR	KxR
33	R-B6ch	K-K2	39	BxB	PxB
34	R-N3	B-N3	40	K-N1	Resigns

MATING SACRIFICES

As has been shown, the sacrifice for gain and the mating sacrifice are similar in nature. In both cases we have the realization, by violent means, of an advantage, be it permanent or temporary.

The permanent advantage, built up on the Pawn formation, is strategical; the temporary advantage, based on the configuration of the pieces at a given moment, is tactical. For our purpose the tactical advantage is more important, for the sacrifice—especially the sham sacrifice—is as a rule a tactical weapon. Sacrificing opportunities are usually fleeting and must be seized at the right moment. This is particularly the case when the positional advantage is purely tactical. Where the advantage is strategical and therefore enduring, it sometimes happens that the opportunity for sacrificing remains open for a number of moves or recurs at different times.

But whereas the sacrifice for gain only aims at material benefit and after its consummation leaves the opponent still able to show fight or at least put up some resistance, the object of the mating sacrifice is to terminate the game there and then.

The mating sacrifice is therefore the strongest of all sacrifices and justifies the biggest stake. It is not a question of regaining material but of forcing checkmate—a consideration which outweighs all others.

The notion that the mating sacrifice is only a sham sacrifice may strike the student as strange, but it is logical enough: the sacrifice is offered for a limited, well-defined period of time; the attacker runs no risk, and so the real character of a sacrifice does not obtain.

Broadly speaking, the attacker must already have a vastly superior position when he embarks on a mating sacrifice. Marked predominance either in position or in development— often in both—is an essential condition. The cases are rare, however, in which the mate can actually be enforced; more often than not the defender can ward off the mate by incurring the heaviest material losses. But this is only of academic interest. Faced with the alternative of "mate or loss of a Rook," no sensible player will continue the game. We all know the oft-recurring formula: "Resigns, as mate or heavy material loss cannot be avoided.'

EXAMPLE 6

Caro-Kann Defense
Match, 1929

WHITE	BLACK	WHITE	BLACK
R. Spielmann	B. Hönlinger	R. Spielmann	B. Hönlinger
1 P-K4	P-QB3	5 N-N3	P-K3
2 P-Q4	P-Q4	6 N-B3	P-B4
3 N-QB3	PxP	7 B-Q3	N-B3
4 NxP	N-B3	8 PxP	BxP
		9 P-QR3	. . . .

[Preserves his King Bishop on its attacking diagonal by preventing . . . N-QN5, and prepares for P-N4 creating an attacking diagonal for the other Bishop.]

9	....	O-O	11	P-N4	B-K2
10	O-O	P-QN3	12	B-N2	Q-B2?

Weak, as he does not prevent N-K5 after all. 12 . . . B-N2 is much better.

13 P-N5   N-QR4

Better 13 . . . N-N1 and if 14 B-K5, Q-Q2!

14 N-K5   B-N2

Preferable is 14 . . . N-N2 followed by . . . N-B4 etc.

15 N-N4   . . . .

[Threatening to win quickly by breaking up Black's King-side.]

15 . . . .   Q-Q1

He should try 15 . . . Q-KB5.

16 N-K3!   N-Q4?

16 . . . R-B1 is in order. The text leads to delightful sacrificial possibilities.

In this position White boasts of by far the better development. True, only the minor pieces are mobilized, but the

White forces are trained on the hostile King-side, while of the Black pieces some are ineffectually, some badly, placed. This latter applies particularly to the Knight on R4.

In a purely positional sense, Black is very well placed, as White's Queen Bishop Pawn is backward. Black's last move is a premature attempt to emphasize his positional prospects. He would indeed have excellent chances if he could only find time for . . . B-KB3; for which reason the position is not without danger for the first player as well.

Quick and energetic action is required. Black's 16 . . . N-Q4? gives White his opportunity; for while . . . B-KB3 is threatened, it weakens, on the other hand, that part of the board which was already in danger. Thus White can opportunely throw his most powerful piece into the fray with decisive effect.

17   Q-R5!   P-N3

Apart from this move, only 17 . . . P-KR3 and 17 . . . P-B4 are to be considered.

If 17 . . . P-KR3; 18 BxP!, KxB; 19 N-B5ch, PxN; 20 NxPch followed by mate in a few moves.

If 17 . . . P-B4; 18 NxP!, PxN; 19 NxP, N-KB3; 20 Q-N5!, P-N3; 21 KR-K1, B-B4; 22 R-K6 and wins, for example 22 . . . Q-Q4; 23 N-R6ch, K-N2; 24 RxN!, QxQ; 25 RxP mate!

[Note these examples of mating sacrifices.]

18   N-N4!   . . . .

This mating sacrifice is the point of the Queen move. It is passive in the sense that it can be declined, but nevertheless it leads to a considerable weakening of the enemy's power of resistance.

18 ....   B-KB3

The only defense against the threat of 19 N-R6 mate. 18 . . . P-B3 fails against 19 BxNP, PxB; 20 QxPch, K-R1; 21 N-R5.

18 . . . N-KB3 is completely refuted by 19 Q-K5, K-N2 (if 19 . . . Q-Q4; 20 QxQ! wins a piece); 20 NxN, BxN; 21 N-R5ch!, PxN; 22 Q-N5ch, K-R1; 23 Q-R6 etc.

19 NxBch   NxN

Or 19 . . . QxN; 20 BxQ, PxQ; 21 NxP and the endgame is won for White.

20 Q-R6   ....

Not 20 Q-K5, when Black forces the exchange of Queens with 20 . . . Q-Q4!

The success of the proffered Queen sacrifice is now patent: Black's King Bishop has disappeared, whereby White's Bishop at N2 has gained enormously in power.

20	R-B1	21 QR-Q1	Q-K2
		22 KR-K1	....

Threatens to win at once by 23 N-B5.

| 22 .... | N-K1 | 23 N-B5! | .... |

He plays it anyway! The idea is that after 23 . . . NPxN; 24 BxP, P-B3; 25 BxKPch, K-R1; 26 R-Q7 wins.

$$23 \quad \dots \quad \text{Q-B4}$$

If 23 . . . Q-B2 there is a pretty finish by 24 B-B6! threatening to win the Queen by 25 N-K7ch, as neither the Knight at B5 nor the Bishop at B6 can be captured; nor can Black's K2 receive any reinforcements.

$$24 \quad \text{R-K5} \qquad \text{B-Q4}$$

After 24 . . . Q-B2 White wins in the same manner.

Now follows a typical instance of an active mating sacrifice.

$$25 \quad \text{N-K7ch!} \qquad \text{Resigns}$$

The last move was a vacating sacrifice, which we shall discuss at length later on. We are dealing here with a sham sacrifice. If Black captures the Knight—and he must—the mating sacrifice then follows: 26 QxRPch, KxQ; 27 R-R5ch (this is why the rank had to be vacated for the Rook), K-N1; 28 R-R8 mate.

EXAMPLE 7

Sicilian Defense
Marienbad, 1925

WHITE	BLACK	WHITE	BLACK
	Dr. S.		Dr. S.
R. Spielmann	Tartakover	R. Spielmann	Tartakover
1 P-K4	P-QB4	3 P-Q4	PxP
2 N-KB3	P-K3	4 NxP	P-QR3

[Too cramping, as White's reply demonstrates. Better 4 . . . N-KB3 inducing 5 N-QB3 when White's grip on the center is less marked than in the actual play.]

5	P-QB4!	N-KB3	11	R-B1	P-QN3
6	N-QB3	Q-B2	12	P-QN4	B-N2
7	P-QR3!	B-K2	13	P-B3	QR-B1
8	B-K2	O-O	14	Q-K1!	Q-N1
9	O-O	P-Q3	15	Q-B2	B-Q1
10	B-K3	QN-Q2	16	N-R4	N-K4
			17	N-N2	P-Q4?

Black's pieces are not favorably placed for the extensive opening-up of the game which this move involves. 17 . . . B-B2 is in order.

18	KPxP	PxP	20	NxN	PxN
19	N-B5!	NxP	21	BxBP	Q-K4

A better defense is 21 . . . P-QN4; 22 B-Q3, RxR; 23 RxR, B-B1; 24 B-B5, BxN; 25 BxB, R-K1 although White remains with the advantage of the two Bishops.

22	B-Q3	RxR	24	B-Q4	Q-B5
23	RxR	N-Q4	25	R-K1	B-KB3
			26	BxB	PxB?

A more protracted resistance is possible after 26 . . . NxB, despite the loss of the Queen Knight Pawn.

27   P-N3   Q-B2

Or 27 . . . Q-N4; 28 P-KR4; Q-R4; 29 P-N4 and White wins the Queen.

28 Q-Q2   Q-B6

White has much the better of it in every respect. The bad position of Black's King allows a mating attack which happens to be bound up with a sacrifice.

This sacrifice is part of the actual mating operations only in the sense of gaining the essential tempo for avoiding the exchange of Queens without having to stop to guard the Rook.

29 Q-R6!   QxRch

Dr. Tartakover, always ready for his little joke, insists on "being shown."

30 B-B1   R-K1

31 Q-N7 mate

A primitive example.

EXAMPLE 8

Queen's Gambit Accepted
Carlsbad, 1929

WHITE	BLACK	WHITE	BLACK
R. Spielmann	E. Grünfeld	R. Spielmann	E. Grünfeld
1 P-Q4	P-Q4	2 P-QB4	P-K3
		3 N-QB3	PxP

Not a good way of accepting the gambit, as P-K4 can follow with good effect. *[White gets a much freer game.]*

4 P-K4!	P-QB4	8 O-O	N-QB3
5 N-B3	PxP	9 N-B3!	Q-B2
6 NxP	P-QR3	10 Q-K2	B-Q3
7 BxP	B-Q2	11 R-Q1	. . . .

Preventing 11 . . . N-B3. *[For if 11 . . . N-B3; 12 RxB!, QxR; 13 P-K5 etc.]*

11	KN-K2	13 NxN	BxN
12 B-K3	N-K4	14 P-KN3	BxN

In order to close the Queen Bishop file, as the threat of QR-B1 was very strong.

15 PxB	N-N3	16 B-N3	O-O

Not 16 . . . QxP because of 17 B-Q4.

17 B-Q4   P-N4?

An ill-conceived plan. 17 . . . P-K4 is also inferior because of 18 B-N6, QxB; 19 RxB. Best is 16 . . . B-B3 although White still has the better game because of his two Bishops.

18 Q-K3   B-B3   19 P-KR4!   Q-N2?

Complementing 17 . . . P-N4? but the move is a fatal mistake. 19 . . . P-R3 is indispensable.

20 P-R5   N-K2

White has now a clear win because of the momentary weakness of Black's KN2, which can be additionally attacked by Queen and King Rook Pawn. But the situation must be exploited at once, as otherwise Black can safeguard his position and then rely on his superior Pawn formation. In that event White's Bishops would no more than equalize matters.

21 BxNP!   . . . .

An active mating sacrifice true to type: it forces mate or such ruinous loss of material that further resistance is useless.

Another decisive line was 21 Q-N5, P-B3; 22 BxPch, K-R1;

23 P-R6! (another mating sacrifice); but the text continuation is even stronger.

21 ....   KxB

Accepting the sacrifice leads to a forced mate, but there is no playable method of declining. The threat was 22 B-B6 rather than 22 BxR, thus: 21 . . . BxP; 22 B-B6, B-R8; 23 B-Q5! etc.

22 Q-N5ch   N-N3   23 P-R6ch   ....

The point: if 23 . . . K-N1; 24 Q-B6 followed by mate. The attack against Black's KN2 has won through.

Black resigns.

EXAMPLE 9

French Defense
Magdeburg, 1927

WHITE	BLACK	WHITE	BLACK
R. Spielmann	R. L'hermet	R. Spielmann	R. L'hermet
1 P-K4	P-K3	4 NxP	N-Q2
2 P-Q4	P-Q4	5 N-KB3	KN-B3
3 N-Q2	PxP	6 NxNch	NxN
		7 B-Q3	P-KR3?

Preparing for . . . B-Q3, but both moves are weak. *[Black prevents B-N5, but he creates a target for White's subsequent P-KN4-5.]* Rubinstein's 7 . . . P-QN3 is probably best.

8 Q-K2   B-Q3?   9 B-Q2   O-O

He should endeavor to castle on the other wing.

10 O-O-O	B-Q2	11 N-K5	P-B4
		12 PxP!	....

12	....	BxN

Black already has a lost game. If 12 . . . BxP; 13 P-KN4!
etc. *[The drawbacks of 7 . . . P-KR3? are already becoming
noticeable.]*

13	QxB	B-B3	16	B-Q6	Q-K1
14	B-KB4	Q-K2	17	KR-N1	P-QN3
15	Q-Q4!	KR-Q1	18	Q-KR4	PxP
			19	B-K5!	....

Much stronger than maintaining the Pawn ahead.

19	....	Q-K2?

He should have tried 19 . . . N-Q2.

20	P-KN4	P-B5

Hoping to weaken the attack by exchanging Rooks.

21	P-N5!	N-Q2

21 . . . PxB; 22 PxN is hopeless for Black—likewise 21 . . .
PxP; 22 QxNP.

21 . . . N-R2 is refuted by 22 BxNch, KxB; 23 P-N6ch
winning the Queen.

[See diagram on page 38.]

It is clear at a glance that this position must be won for White. But both of his Bishops are *en prise;* hence a brisk solution is in order. There are several such, of which the following is doubtless the best.

22   QxRP!   . . . .

22 BxNP—likewise a mating sacrifice—also wins quickly, as does 22 B-R7ch, K-B1; 23 BxPch. But the text sacrifice, based on a definite idea, is probably the most forcing. Mate is threatened in two ways and there is no worthwhile way to decline the offer.

| 22 . . . . | PxQ | 23 | PxPdis ch | K-B1 |
| | | 24 | R-N8ch! | . . . . |

The joker. Mate in two follows: 24 . . . KxR; 25 P-R7ch, K-B1; 26 P-R8 (Q or R) mate.
Black resigns.

This concludes our treatment of sham sacrifices.
Before proceeding further, let us pause for a brief résumé.
Sham sacrifices are transitory combinations and must therefore be calculated from the very first move to the end.
Positional sacrifices aim at an abstract benefit (improved position); sacrifices for gain and mating sacrifices have concrete objects (capture of material or checkmate).

Positional sacrifices operate at the beginning of the struggle, as a rule in the opening or as the middle game develops.

Sacrifices for gain form the line of demarcation between the creative and technical parts of a game; they appear towards the end of the actual contest.

Mating sacrifices are conclusive combinations and form the climax as well as the final stage of a game of chess.

With positional sacrifices the player sets himself the task—by no means irrevocable—of turning a possibly infinitesimal advantage into a win. They are often accompanied by an increase both in the number and difficulty of problems to be solved.

Sacrifices for gain greatly ease a player's problems, for they decide the issue and merely impose the responsibility of following up the beaten foe in an appropriate manner.

Mating combinations are the crowning-point of our labors and conclude our task.

Every sacrifice, of whatever type, is only made possible by some mistake on the adversary's part; but this is not to say that the mistake must necessarily be followed at once by the sacrifice. Normally some slight delinquency will be followed by a positional sacrifice; whereas a bad mistake should give opportunities for a sacrifice for gain or a mating sacrifice.

Clearly we must make the reservation that only certain types of mistakes can be exploited by means of a sacrifice. It must be noted also that a number of small faults can ultimately have the same effect as a grievous blunder.

Frequently a mistake only furnishes the premises for a sacrifice which is to be made at a later stage. In this way even some small omission can in certain circumstances lead to a mating sacrifice.

REAL SACRIFICES

The faculty, upon occasion, of converting energy into matter and matter into energy, constitutes one of the most wonderful characteristics of chess, and reveals, perhaps, the innermost secret of its fascination.

The question: "How can I favorably turn matter into energy?" occurs as a rule in the early part of the game; the converse is more likely to obtain for the later phase. We are now concerned with the transformation of matter into energy —the sacrifice of material for the sake of dynamic advantages.

The sacrifices in the first group were based on such substantial dynamic superiority that the conversion of matter into power was followed by the forced reconversion of power into matter. This is also true of mating sacrifices, where it is a question of subduing the hostile King.

Now we are to encounter *real* sacrifices, those which are characterized by the element of risk. Though the concrete benefit can be assumed with a certain degree of probability, it cannot be counted on with absolute reliability.

Real sacrifices, in contradistinction to sham sacrifices, are not combinations in the ordinary sense, but rather combinations *with a time factor.*

The likelihood of success is not necessarily based on positional judgment alone; it may be dependent on various extraneous circumstances. It is possible, for example, to allow for an opponent's individual failings: to play psychologically.

Or one can speculate on his time-difficulties, taking a sporting chance. Considered in this light, many combinations can be termed correct in a broader sense even though they may not be able to stand the test of subsequent analysis. We must distinguish between *practical* and *theoretical* soundness.

The critic, of course, is very rarely in a position to give due weight to these important factors. As a rule only the players themselves can give information on these matters—another argument in support of my decision to give only my own games as illustrations.

SACRIFICES FOR DEVELOPMENT

The simplest of the real sacrifices is that for development. The material given up consists usually of one or two Pawns, on rare occasions three Pawns or even a piece or two. The object is to out-distance your opponent in development. A more definite purpose, or any intention to recover the material given up, does not obtain for the time being. The argument runs: "If only I am ahead in development, favorable attacking chances will arise of themselves."

Sacrifices for development occur, in the nature of things, in the opening or the early middle game, that part of the game in which the players contend for development. We are familiar with many such sacrifices, so characteristic of the gambit openings. We are also familiar with the rule of thumb to the effect that three developing moves are approximately worth a Pawn. This may be near enough to the truth, but, generally speaking, this applies only to open positions. In close games in which there is no immediate chance of opening up lines, it is imperative to be much more circumspect in sacrificing for development. A point always to be considered is whether the Pawn formations are mobile or interlocked. In this respect the situation in the center will always be the prevailing factor. A numerically superior Pawn center, linked up with a better, or at least equal, development of the pieces, offers favorable prospects of attack because it facilitates the opening of lines.

I cannot stress too strongly a warning note against that type of center which is fundamentally weak, despite its numerical strength, because it lacks the essential support of the pieces. The fact that this "strong" center is actually a weakness was not properly appraised by the older masters, who were thus handicapped in the fight "classics versus moderns."

To recapitulate: where sacrifices for development are concerned, what really matters is quick development rather than the formation of a strong center—which latter, although a favorable concomitant, is not an essential, not an end in itself.

The two following examples illustrate sacrifices for development such as occur frequently in practical play. The games are not in themselves of much value; but that is not of great moment in this book. If the particular kind of sacrifice is clearly demonstrated, the object is achieved.

EXAMPLE 10

Ruy Lopez
Scheveningen, 1905

WHITE	BLACK	WHITE	BLACK
G. Schories	R. Spielmann	G. Schories	R. Spielmann
1 P-K4	P-K4	5 O-O	NxP
2 N-KB3	N-QB3	6 P-Q4	P-QN4
3 B-N5	P-QR3	7 B-N3	P-Q4
4 B-R4	N-B3	8 PxP	B-K3

[Spielmann was fond of this defense because of its aggressive character. In Example 33 we have another instance of his play with this line.]

9 P-B3	B-QB4	11 Q-K2	O-O
10 P-QR4	P-N5	12 B-B2	. . . .

Black is threatened with the loss of a Pawn, as his Knight on K5 is attacked twice. This Knight can be supported by 12 . . . B-B4; no further attack on the Knight need be feared because 13 QN-Q2? is refuted by 13 . . . NxQBP! and 13 N-N5 can be answered quite satisfactorily by 13 . . . NxN; 14 BxB, N-K3 followed by . . . P-Q5. Hence White has to answer 12 . . . B-B4 with 13 B-K3 with about an even game.

Thus it is clear that Black can defend the position in a sound if commonplace manner. Yet the situation seems to call for a Pawn sacrifice: for if White captures twice on his K4, he loses time, gives up his best attacking piece (the King Bishop), exposes his Queen and leaves his opponent with the two Bishops. In addition, Black, in the position of the diagram, is a tempo ahead—though this is momentarily set off by White's superior Pawn formation.

Let us consider what would happen if it were White's move and he decided to carry out his threat: 13 BxN, PxB; 14 QxKP, B-Q4; 15 Q-K2, BxN and now if White wishes to conserve his extra Pawn, he must break up his King-side with 16 PxB, and his position is anything but enviable. As Black has a move before all this happens, it seems plausible for him to disregard the threat and continue to build up his position; perhaps in such a way that, in order to win the Pawn, White will have to open a file for Black's Rooks. There we have it, we are on the right track!

12 .... P-B4

Now White is faced with a difficult problem: he must either concede the consolidation of Black's position at K5 and thus admit his move 12 B-B2 was defective; or else he must go on with the Pawn-winning expedition, whereby he neglects his development and substantially promotes that of his opponent.

13 PxP e.p. ....

And so White decides to accept the offer. He may have been influenced in this decision by the fact that the tranquil continuation 13 B-K3—the only alternative worth considering— also fails to inspire confidence. The sequel might be: 13 . . . BxB; 14 QxB, P-B5; 15 Q-Q3,B-B4; or 15 Q-K2, B-N5. In either case White is far from happy.

13 .... QxP

Black is splendidly developed and must obtain a strong attack no matter how play proceeds.

14 BxN ....

White might just as well accept the sacrifice, as a quiet continuation (14 B-K3, B-Q3) leaves Black with the advantage and no risk involved.

14 .... PxB　15 QxKP　B-N6

Protecting the Black Knight, preventing White's Queen from reaching her QB2 and also preventing a possible Q-B4ch at a later stage. Black has secured a very promising and menacing game which, however, he has yet to win.

[See diagram on page 45.]

16 P-B4? ....

Just as the battle between the numerically superior side and

the better-developed forces is about to begin, the defender (White) makes a mistake which tips the scales clearly in the attacker's favor. "Then," many will say, "this game is a poor one, and of little use as an example." On the contrary! The game is a good illustration precisely because of the mistake. For it is a *typical* mistake.

Practical play adduces evidence that errors occur far more frequently in defense than in attack. This is particularly the case when the defender has to solve unusual problems. In this game the unusual problem is that not only the lack of development is to be remedied, but that the material advantage is to be preserved at the same time. It would not be satisfactory to expedite development by giving back the Pawn, for Black would still have his two Bishops. Though the task was possibly not insuperable, it was certainly one of extreme difficulty.

For over the board the moral effect of the attack plays an important role. This effect, experience teaches us, is particularly acute after a sacrifice. The reasons are technical as well as psychological. The attacker's troops are well deployed for the battle, he commands great freedom of space, he can carry out lightning changes of venue and of tactics, and in consequence, besides the main object, he can pursue all kinds of subsidiary schemes. The defender is limited to striving to see through his opponent's plans and often he can only guess their purpose. At best he can espy some flaw in the enemy front. This task requires far more care and willpower than the attack, is therefore far more taxing and frequently leads to a weakening of the power of resistance: either the problem becomes too difficult or all faith in the position is lost.

In the position of the diagram White should at least try to develop with B-K3 and QN-Q2. In that case also, Black maintains the attack: 16 B-K3, QR-K1; 17 Q-Q3, B-Q3; 18 QN-Q2, N-K4; if now 19 QxP??, NxNch; 20 NxN, BxPch and White's Queen is lost.

The text move (16 P-B4?) is due to an all too ambitious scheme to shut out and eventually win Black's Queen Bishop.

16   ....   Q-Q3

This move parries the threats of 17 Q-Q5ch and 17 Q-Q3, and at the same time prepares an attack on the Queen Bishop Pawn should White show any intention of exchanging Bishops: 17 B-K3, QR-K1; 18 BxB, QxB etc. White should nevertheless choose this variation, giving back the Pawn and exchanging Queens by 19 Q-Q5ch, in order to seek not impossible chances of salvation in the endgame.

17 QN-Q2?   QR-K1   18 Q-N1   ....

Now Black's Queen Bishop is firmly trapped; but White fails to realize that he will never have an opportunity to capture the prisoner. However, even 18 Q-Q5ch does not bring relief: 18 . . . QxQ; 19 PxQ, BxQP; and Black with his excellent development, his two Bishops and Queen-side Pawn majority, has a clearly won game.

18   ....   N-Q5!

Beginning the final assault. (In playing 16 P-QB4?, White overlooked that he was seriously weakening his Q4.)

Already there is a sham sacrifice in the air: 19 NxN, QxN; 20 NxB, QxPch! followed by mate. This possibility requires no intricate calculations—with a development so much superior, such variations occur almost of their own accord. The move in the text also threatens to win a piece by 19 . . . B-B7 and 20 . . . P-N6. White is lost and what follows is desperation.

19	N-K4	NxNch	20	PxN	Q-N3ch
			21	K-R1	RxP!

A mating sacrifice: if 22 NxB, B-B7; 23 Q-R2, RxP with a forced mate.

22	R-K1	RxP	24	N-B6ch	PxN
23	B-N5	Q-R4	25	RxRch	K-B2
				Resigns	

EXAMPLE 11

Queen's Gambit Declined
Ostend, 1906

WHITE	BLACK	WHITE	BLACK
Dr. O. S.		Dr. O. S.	
Bernstein	R. Spielmann	Bernstein	R. Spielmann
1 P-Q4	P-Q4	3 N–QB3	P-QB4
2 P-QB4	P-K3	4 BPxP	KPxP
		5 PxP	

Much stronger is the line subsequently introduced by Schlechter and Rubinstein: 5 N-B3, N-QB3; 6 P-KN3 followed by 7 B-N2.

5	P-Q5	7 NxB	Q-R4ch
6 N-R4	BxP	8 Q-Q2?	....

An unfortunate plan. Black's Queen Pawn, on which White

wishes to concentrate, is too strong and a thankless object for attack. 8 B-Q2 was indicated.

8	....	QxN	11	P-QR3	B-K3
9	P-QN4	Q-N3	12	N-B3	R-Q1
10	B-N2	N-QB3	13	Q-N5?	....

White should develop with P-K3 or P-KN3 etc. The Queen move is too labored to be good.

White's situation is quite uncomfortable. Black's Queen Pawn exerts pressure on his game and cannot very well be eliminated. The Queen's raid, undertaken with the King-side undeveloped, was made to gain time, and would be justified by the achievement of that goal.

But is it reasonably possible to hinder Black's sound plans by such abnormal means? Most unlikely! There arises the question, therefore, how White would stand if allowed to capture the King Knight Pawn (this being the threat by which he hoped to gain time). And with this the problem is already solved: not the Pawn, but rather the King Rook which is also menaced, has to be guarded. Hence the sacrifice for development:

13   ....   N-B3!   14   QxP?

It was better to play for the exchange of Queens with 14 Q-QB5; the ensuing endgame might be tenable. The text move is consistent but foolhardy.

14 .... K-K2

The sacrifice is already vindicated: Black has a terrific lead in development. With halfway suitable play, he must obtain a violent attack before White can make up for the time lost. This will be all the easier to accomplish as White's Queen-side offers an easy mark. In fact, 15 ... NxP is already threatened, which explains White's next move.

15 Q-R6　　KR-N1　　16 R-Q1　　P-R4

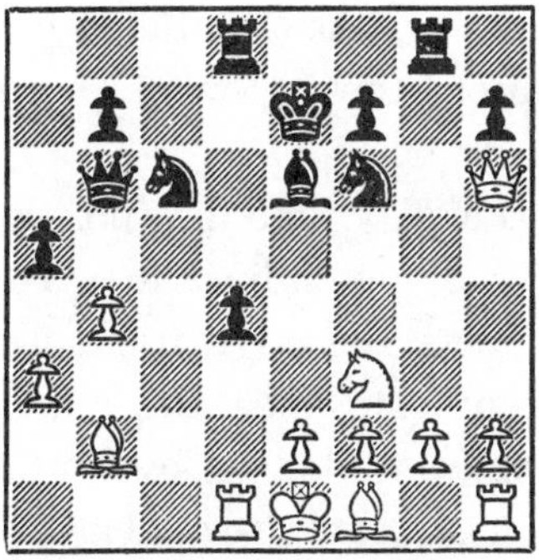

The attack now wins through with utmost ease. At one or two points there are even several lines to choose from—another proof of Black's marked superiority.

17	Q-Q2	N-K5	21	B-B1	R-Q3
18	Q-B2	P-B4	22	P-B3	N-B6
19	PxP	QxPch	23	P-N3	R-QN3
20	N-Q2	N-K4	24	K-B2	R-QB1

Now White's Queen, which has no flight square, is threatened with a discovery [25 ... N—K5ch]. It is evident how wise it was for Black not to be content with a gain in material.

25 K-N1 ....

An oversight, but there was nothing to be done, as White suffers a disastrous loss of material.

25 .... NxKPch

White resigns.

In these two examples, it was actually the respective opponents who seized the initiative and thereby created the opportunity of a counter-sacrifice for development. However, this course of events is typical of its kind and can be observed in frequent instances other than well-known gambits.

From this the conclusion must be drawn that the utmost circumspection is called for before venturing on attacking Pawns, or even pieces, when one's development is still uncompleted. In any event, it is essential to probe whether or not such attacks will afford the opponent an opportunity of making a promising sacrifice.

If the defender is at any time in a position to disregard the attack, and, instead of defending, to make a developing or even an attacking move, the original attacker will find himself in a painful quandary. He must either admit that his attack was ill-conceived and only led to loss of time, or, against his will—for after all, he meant to attack!—resign himself to a wearisome defense. Examples 10 and 11 both illustrate this point. In one, Schories plays 12 B-B2, hoping to keep his opponent occupied, but is baffled by a sacrifice; in the other, Bernstein has a very similar experience after the mistakenly intended gain of a tempo by 13 Q-N5.

OBSTRUCTIVE SACRIFICES

As mentioned in the Introduction, this sacrifice is akin to the sacrifice for development. At any rate, both have the same object: to get ahead in development. But the respective ways and means are different. With the obstructive sacrifice the attacker attempts to hold up the enemy's development. This course definitely demands more action than does the simple sacrifice for development.

The attacker cannot merely let things depend, for instance, on whether or not the opponent will capture a proffered Pawn; he must, on the contrary, *exercise compulsion*. It follows that obstructive sacrifices are always active: they cannot be declined without disadvantage. As a rule they involve the sacrifice of no more than a Pawn. If greater values are staked, some partial compensation in material must be secured.

Herein lies an important and relevant distinction between the sacrifice for development and the obstructive sacrifice. With the first, in the ordinary course of events, the attacker continues his development regardless of attacks on his own Pawns. If the opponent captures the material offered, he loses time. The attacker bases his calculations on this fact.

It is otherwise in the case of the obstructive sacrifice. Here the attacker gives up not only material but time as well. His own development derives no immediate benefit from the sacrifice, which actually decreases the number of forces which he has actively participating in the struggle. It follows that an obstructive sacrifice can only be a paying proposition where the object can be achieved with a minimum stake. Problem-like positions turn up on occasion, but they are exceptions.

As a rule the obstructive sacrifice will have to be of such a nature that its effect will be felt principally in the center. For the center is the junction of all the lines of development, and any obstruction set up there will be felt first.

EXAMPLE 12

Alekhine's Defense
Match, 1933

WHITE	BLACK	WHITE	BLACK
R. Spielmann	S. Landau	R. Spielmann	S. Landau
1 P-K4	N-KB3	2 N-QB3	P-Q4

It is best, in my opinion, to lead into the Vienna Game with
2 . . . P-K4.

3   P-K5   KN-Q2

After 3 . . . P-Q5 (or 3 . . . N-K5); 4 QN-K2! I prefer
White's position.

In this position Black threatens to branch off into a favorable variation of the French Defense by playing 4 . . . P-K3.
In that case the White Knight at QB3 would be poorly placed,
as it blocks the Queen Bishop Pawn which, logically, should
advance to QB3.

White can avoid this variation by 4 NxP, but then 4 . . . NxP
gives a level game. Hence the following sacrifice, which enables White to maintain the initiative which is his birthright.

4   P-K6!   . . . .

The obstructive sacrifice in its simplest and most familiar
form! White offers a Pawn, and a tempo as well. The tempo,
however, is of little moment, as Black is compelled to accept
and thus loses time also.

The Black Pawn which will now occupy White's K6 is a
"block," in problemists' parlance. First of all, it prevents Black
from consolidating his position against attack by playing . . .
P-K3. In principle this favors the attack. Further, the development of Black's Queen and both Bishops is sadly hampered,
and in the absence of a Pawn at KB2 the King's Field is much

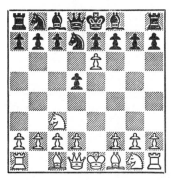

weakened. In addition, the extra Pawn is itself a weakness, being backward on an open file.

In these circumstances, and on the assumption that Black will try to preserve his Pawn, White will subsequently be able to proceed uninterruptedly with his development, whereas Black will be able to marshal his forces—after a fashion—only with the greatest difficulty. On the whole, a sacrifice full of promise.

| 4 .... | PxP | 5 P-Q4 | N-KB3 |

After this move, Black's development will soon arrive at a deadlock. It is the development of the Bishops, not of the Knights, that should concern him. To this end the counter-sacrifice 5 . . . P-K4 was called for, so that if 6 PxP (not 6 NxP, PxP; 7 QxP?, N-N3! followed by . . . P-B3 winning a piece), P-K3 with a much less arduous defense.

| 6 N-B3 | P-B4 |

He is already at a loss. The counter-sacrifice of the Queen Bishop Pawn remains ineffectual because it does not strike at the root of the evil, the shutting-in of the Bishops. The plan of advancing . . . P-K4 in safety is altogether too ambitious to be practicable.

| 7 PxP | N-B3 |

Here also, even at the cost of a Pawn, . . . P-K4 followed
by . . . P-K3 was the best course.

8 B-QN5!   . . . .

Permanently obstructing the advance . . . P-K4, and this
alone is enough to assure a decisive advantage.

| 8 . . . . | B-Q2 | 9 O-O | Q-B2 |
| | | 10 R-K1 | P-KR3 |

The Pawn at K3 is not only an obstruction; it begins to be a
weakness as well. White was threatening 11 N-N5.

| 11 BxN | PxB | 12 N-K5 | P-N4 |
| | | 13 Q-Q3 | KR-N1 |

Sacrificing the exchange by 13 . . . O-O-O was preferable;
on the next move, . . . O-O-O would make a longer resistance
possible.

| 14 P-QN4 | B-N2 | 15 Q-N6ch | K-Q1 |
| | | 16 Q-B7 | . . . . |

Threatening 17 NxB and 18 RxP, beginning the harvest.
Anticipating this, Black tries a counter-combination which
proves unsound.

| 16 . . . . | B-K1 | 17 QxP | R-KB1 |
| | | 18 P-N5 | N-K5 |

Black's last hope, 18 . . . N-N5 being refuted by 19 NxP!
The text move looks very strong.

[*See diagram on page 55.*]

19 RxN!   PxR

Nothing is gained by 19 . . . BxN; 20 RxB, R-B3—which
fails because of 21 RxPch!

20 B-B4!   . . . .

The point of the sacrifice. Both sacrifices reveal themselves as interrelated vacating sacrifices. The Queen file was opened with gain of tempo and now the first rank is cleared. There is no defense against the threatened intervention of the Queen Rook.

| 20 | .... | BxN | 22 | R-Q1 | PxP |
| 21 | BxB | Q-Q2 | 23 | RxQch | .... |

Even stronger was 23 P-B6!

| 23 | .... | BxR | 25 | P-B6 | B-K1 |
| 24 | QxP | KR-N1 | 26 | NxNP | Resigns |

The consequences of an obstructive sacrifice are shown particularly clearly in this game. Once White has hemmed in his opponent by P-K6, his immediate task consists solely in maintaining the blockade by normal developing moves. In this way his pieces will quite automatically develop far superior efficacy. Given these circumstances, a despairing sortie by the second player only hastened the decision. Black's fundamental mistake is that he makes no attempt to raise the central blockade, if need be by violent means (counter-sacrifice . . . P-K4). In consequence, his forces remain scattered and he cannot withstand the enemy's concentrated assault.

EXAMPLE 13

Queen's Gambit Accepted
(in effect)
Vienna, 1933

WHITE	BLACK	WHITE	BLACK
R. Spielmann	B. Hönlinger	R. Spielmann	B. Hönlinger
1 P-K4	P-QB3	5 N-QB3	P-K3
2 P-Q4	P-Q4	6 N-B3	PxP
3 PxP	PxP	7 BxP	B-K2
4 P-QB4	N-KB3	8 O-O	O-O
		9 B-B4	P-QR3

9 . . . QN-Q2 is better.

10 P-Q5!	PxP	12 BxKN	N-Q2
11 NxP	NxN	13 Q-B2!	. . . .

Avoiding the exchange of Queens.

13 . . . .   Q-R4

Better 13 . . . N-B3 and 14 . . . B-KN5.

14 B-QN3   N-B4   15 QR-K1   . . . .

In order to answer 15 . . . NxB with 16 RxB!

15 . . . .   Q-Q1

16 R-Q1   Q-N3   17 B-N5!   BxB

Else 17 . . . B-Q3; 18 B-K3! etc.; or 17 . . . NxB?; 18 BxB.

18 NxB   P-N3

White's attack seems to be petering out, as the liberating moves . . . NxB and . . . B-B4 apparently cannot be prevented. But Black's development is not yet completed, and a small sacrifice by White forces it to remain that way.

19	BxPch!	RxB	20	NxR	KxN
			21	R-Q5!	....

The point of the combination. The attacked Knight must retreat either to Q2 or K3. In either case he hems in the Bishop, which in turn obstructs the Rook so that, at a stroke, White is able to attack the denuded King with overwhelming power. The capture at KB7 is thus revealed to be an obstructive sacrifice. The sacrifice is small quantitatively, for Rook and Pawn for Knight and Bishop is equivalent, mathematically speaking, to the loss of only half a Pawn. (See the section on "Sacrificial Values.")

But, other things being equal, the two pieces are undoubtedly stronger, especially when the major pieces are still on the board. Knight and Bishop are much better fitted for the attack than Rook and Pawn; and for the time being the Pawn is of no account. [*White's sacrifice, then, is not quite so "small" as our modest author has described it.*]

21 .... N-K3

After 21 ... N-Q2 White can choose between 22 Q-B4 and 22 KR-Q1.

22 KR-Q1 Q-B3

Black has no satisfactory move. Knight moves are answered by 23 R-Q8 etc.

23 Q-N3   P-QN4   24 R-Q6   Q-K5

25 Q-B3!   . . . .

Preventing the enemy from developing is the attacker's most important task after an obstructive sacrifice. The text move prevents 25 . . . B-N2, to which the answer would be 26 P-B3 winning a piece. Incidentally, 26 Q-R8 etc. is threatened.

25 . . . .   K-K2   26 Q-R8   P-N4

Or 26 . . . QxPch; 27 KxQ, B-N2ch; 28 K-B1, RxQ; 29 R-Q7ch and 30 RxB.

27 P-B3   Q-N3   28 R-Q8!   . . . .

Black has still found no opportunity to catch up in development and is helpless against the hostile assault. If now 28 . . . NxR; 29 QxNch, K-B2; 30 Q-Q5ch and 31 QxR.

28 . . . .   Q-B7   30 Q-N8ch   K-B3
29 R-K8ch   K-B2   31 R-K1   . . . .

An aesthetic flaw. At this point White could have announced mate in five beginning with 31 R-B8ch.

31	Q-B3	32 P-KR4	P-R3

If 32 ... PxP; 33 P-B4 threatening 34 R/K1xNch etc.

	33 P-R5	Resigns	

In this game the second player took desperate risks. Just as safety seemed within his grasp, and the question of equality hung in the balance, the sudden introduction of the sacrifice smashed his plans and decided the issue.

EXAMPLE 14

King's Indian Defense
Match, 1932

WHITE	BLACK	WHITE	BLACK
R. Spielmann	E. Bogolyubov	R. Spielmann	E. Bogolyubov
1 P-Q4	N-KB3	3 P-B3	P-B4
2 P-QB4	P-KN3	4 P-Q5	....

4 PxP followed by 5 P-K4 is also quite good.

4	P-Q3	8 B-K3	P-B5
5 P-K4	P-K4	9 B-KB2	P-KN4
6 B-Q3	N-R4	10 P-KN4	N-KB3
7 N-K2	P-B4	11 P-KR4	PxP
		12 BxRP	P-KR4

Had Bogolyubov won this game, he would still have had a chance of winning the match. Hence the excessively sharp, risky play.

13 P-N5	N-R2?	

13 ... N-N1 was in order.

This position has arisen out of a most uncommon opening. Its peculiarity is immediately apparent. Both sides have made

mostly Pawn moves, particularly the second player, who has only one piece—the King Knight—in play after thirteen moves! In return he does win a Pawn, because now the King Knight Pawn can no longer be held.

White can probably put up with this loss if he continues straightforwardly with N-Q2, Q-B2, O-O-O, relying on his lead in development. The unpleasing factor is that the position as a whole remains barricaded: the extreme King-side is not a good enough basis for successful attack. White therefore tries to think of something better and hits on an unusual obstructive sacrifice in keeping with the character of the position.

14 NxP!   PxN   15 P-K5   B-K2

Black must not capture the King Pawn: 15 . . . PxP; 16 B-N6ch, K-Q2; 17 N-B3 and now there are two threats which cannot both be warded off: (a) 18 BxN, RxB; 19 P-N6, R-K2; 20 P-Q6 etc. and (b) 18 Q-R4ch, K-B2; 19 N-N5ch etc. Note that the parry 17 . . . Q-R4 revives the pending threat of 18 Q-B2 winning the King Knight.

16 P-K6!   . . . .

The real purpose of the sacrifice. After this, all of Black's Queen-side pieces, for a long time to come, will remain excluded from the field of operations. In the meantime, White will develop to his heart's content, and will be able to engineer a violent attack on the badly protected King.

Numerous subsequent examinations have established that this general appraisal of the position was correct: in all cases, a result favorable to White was arrived at. The attacker is able to give up a whole piece—his King Knight Pawn goes lost—in order to obstruct his opponent's development. This is, to be sure, an exceptional case.

Unlike Example 12, in which a defending Pawn provided the block, it is, in this case, the attacker's King Pawn, which moreover is well supported. This type of obstruction is more reliable by far. The defender's King position is so insecure that there is little prospect of a successful counterattack: it would mean opening further lines and this could only be to the attacker's advantage.

16 ....   BxNP

Or 16 ... NxP, which was also playable on the previous move. It would not have altered the general situation; the threat of 17 ... NxPch is comfortably parried by 17 N-Q2.

17   B-KB2   B-B3

The alternative is 17 ... Q-K2; 18 Q-K2, N-Q2; 19 B-N6ch,

K-Q1; 20 PxN, BxP in order to obtain breathing space. **But** then, after 21 B-K4, White has an excellent game.

18   B-N6ch   K-K2

18 ... K-B1 is a little better.

19   N-Q2   N-N4

Capturing at N7 is immediately fatal: 19 ... BxNP; 20 Q-N1, BxR; 21 QxB, N-B3; 22 B-R4 followed eventually by N-K4 and wins—or 20 ... B-B3; 21 BxN, BxR; 22 B-R4ch, B-B3; 23 BxBch, KxB; 24 Q-B5ch and mate in two.

20   Q-B2   R-R3   21   O-O-O   Q-N1

Without the participation of the Queen-side pieces, the defense is quite hopeless. After 21 ... N-Q2; 22 PxN, KxP there was at least some fight left.

22   B-B5   N-R3

Here 22 ... N-Q2 is probably hopeless, as after 23 PxN the King cannot recapture.

23   QR-N1   Q-R1   25   Q-N1   N-R2
24   B-R4   N-N5   26   BxN!   . . . .

26   . . . .   BxB

If Black takes the other Bishop, the sequel is 27 BxBch followed by 28 N-K4ch and 29 R-R4, and the attack romps home.

27	RxB	QxB	28	N-K4	R-N3
			29	N-N5	Q-N2

If 29 . . . Q-R3; 30 Q-B5, R-B3; 31 Q-R7ch (not 31 Q-K4, R-N3), and White wins easily: 31 . . . QxQ; 32 NxQ, R-B4; 33 R-N7ch, K-Q1; 34 RxRP, RxR; 35 P-K7ch, K-Q2; 36 N-B6ch etc.

30	RxRP	P-N4	31	P-R3	N-R7ch

Postponing collapse for a few moves. If 31 . . . N-R3; 32 QR-R1 decides the issue at once.

32	QxN	Q-Q5	33	R-K1	B-R3

If 33 . . . Q-B7; 34 QR-R1—or 33 . . . QxBPch; 34 QxQ, PxQ; 35 R-R7ch followed by 36 N-K4 and White wins in either case.

34	R-R7ch	R-N2	35	RxRch	QxR
			36	Q-N1!	. . . .

Capturing the Knight now leads to mate in four. If 36 . . . R-KN1 (or 36 . . . R-KR1); 37 Q-B5, R-KB1; 38 N-B7 etc.

36	. . . .	PxP	38	RxR	QxR
37	R-R1	R-R1	39	Q-N6	Q-KB1
			40	N-R7!	Resigns

EXAMPLE 15

Caro-Kann Defense
Trentschin-Teplitz, 1928

WHITE	BLACK	WHITE	BLACK
R. Spielmann	M. Walter	R. Spielmann	M. Walter
1 P-K4	P-QB3	4 P-K5	N-K5
2 N-QB3	P-Q4	5 Q-K2	NxN
3 N-B3	N-B3	6 QPxN	P-QN3

Artificial, but by no means fatal. Simplest is 6 . . . P-K3.

7 N-Q4   P-QB4?

The position was fairly even, but Black should at all hazards play 7 . . . P-K3; the text move is entirely illogical. It could only be justified if it promoted the central development of the Queen Bishop (after 8 N-B3) by . . . B-B4 or . . . B-N5. But Black has just played . . . P-QN3 and so stands committed to the fianchetto development of his Queen Bishop.

Therefore, trying to drive the Knight away was, to say the least, ill-timed. In chess, a game of immutable logic, every infringement finds its punishment. Here the retribution is Draconian.

8 P-K6!   . . . .

Two sacrifices at one stroke, one sham and one real! The Knight is offered temporarily, but the Pawn is actually given up. The King Pawn is offered as an obstructive sacrifice which is the real object of the text move. The sacrifice of the Knight is, according to our nomenclature, a sacrifice for gain. If not accepted, it serves the function of lending a helping hand: by staying on at Q4, the Knight makes the obstructive sacrifice possible. As we know, such coordination of several sacrifices is not infrequent. The present case presents a particularly useful example, because a clear-cut distinction can be made as to the type and kind of sacrifice.

Analytically, the text move is based on the following variations:

I. 8 ... PxN?; 9 Q-N5ch, N-Q2 (or 9 ... B-Q2); 10 PxPch, KxP; 11 QxPch followed by 12 QxR.

II. 8 ... B-R3?; 9 Q-N5ch! or 9 QxB! winning at least a piece.

So it appears that neither acceptance of the Knight sacrifice nor counterattack by 8 ... B-R3? is feasible. Black must take the King Pawn with the best grace he can.

8 .... PxP?

Black insists on gaining a tempo by the attack on the Knight. But this capture of the Bishop Pawn is a serious mistake which heightens the effect of the obstructive sacrifice out of all proportion. Clearly 8 ... BxP has to be played, developing a piece and also eliminating White's most aggressive minor piece, as White must reply with 9 NxB.

For the attacker, it is of immeasurable benefit, in positions blocked by a hostile Pawn at K6, to be able to establish a Knight at K5. Concerning this point, compare Example 12 (vs. Landau). With 8 ... BxP Black obviates this contingency.

It was White's intention, in that event, to continue 9 NxB, PxN; 10 B-B4! (The Bishop's move sets the seal on the combination, and is much stronger than 10 QxP, whereupon Black can defend adequately with 10 ... Q-Q2; 11 Q-K3, N-B3.)

The case of a player making a sacrifice and his opponent forthwith responding with a bad mistake is by no means exceptional and is easily explained by the natural effect so imparted. If one wanted to set up a table of probabilities regarding the prospects of a real sacrifice, the effect of surprise would have to rank very high as a factor in favor of success.

9   Q-R5ch   . . . .

Now begins a dreadful holocaust. The obstructive sacrifice hinders the development and coordination of the hostile forces, so that the defending King, as in this instance, has to start a-roving. From the King's travels to the hunting of the King is but a step: one small slip, and—the promenade degenerates into headlong flight.

9   . . . .   K-Q2

Forced. 9 ... P-N3 is answered by 10 Q-K5, R-N1; 11 NxP, BxN; 12 QxB.

   I. 12 ... R-N2; 13 B-N5ch, N-Q2; 14 B-KR6, R-B2; 15 BxB RxB; 16 QxP, R-B1; 17 O-O-O, R-QB2; 18 KR-K1 and White has a clear win.

   II. 12 ... R-R1; 13 B-N5ch, N-Q2; 14 Q-K5!, R-N1; 15 QxP and White wins at once because of the threats 16 QxKR, or 16 BxNch and 17 QxRch.

10   N-B3!   . . . .

Compare the note to Black's eighth move. The effect of the Knight's irruption is catastrophic.

10   . . . .   K-B2

Black has no halfway playable defense. If 10 ... N-B3;

11 B-QN5, B-N2; 12 N-K5ch, K-B2; 13 B-KB4, NxN; 14 QxNch, K-B1; 15 QxPch and mate follows.

11   N-K5   . . . .

11   . . . .   B-Q2

The threat of 12 N-B7 could not be parried:

I. 11 ... P-KN3; 12 NxP, Q-K1; 13 Q-K5ch etc.

II. 11 ... N-Q2; 12 N-B7, Q-K1; 13 B-B4ch, P-K4 (else the Queen is lost by a discovered check); 14 BxPch, NxB; 15 QxNch etc.

III. 11 . . . N-B3; 12 N-B7, Q-K1; 13 B-B4ch, K-Q2; 14 B-QN5, B-N2; 15 N-K5ch and wins.

12	N-B7	Q-K1	14	B-KB4!	P-B5
13	Q-K5ch	K-N2	15	Q-B7ch	K-R3
			16	N-Q8!	. . . .

In order not to miss the opportunity of an inexpensive King-Hunt (see "King-Hunt sacrifice"). 16 NxR would be petty.

16   . . . .   N-B3

Or 16 ... B-B3; 17 Q-B8ch etc.

17   Q-N7ch   K-N4

If 17 ... K-R4; 18 NxNch, BxN; 19 P-N4ch and mate next move.

18   P-R4ch   K-B4

If 18 ... K-R4; 19 NxNch, BxN; 20 P-N4ch, PxP e.p.; 21 Q-R6 mate.

19   QxNch!   BxQ   20   NxP mate

We can now appreciate the vast advantages which can be gained by obstructing the opponent's development. But we have also seen that at times peremptory measures become imperative if pending equalization or even inferiority is to be avoided.

Usually the most propitious moment for an obstructive sacrifice occurs at that stage when the defender takes steps to obtain a full measure of counterplay. As he re-groups his pieces with, perhaps, the assistance of subsidiary threats by which to keep his opponent occupied, his pieces are at times none too secure. This is just the right moment for an attacker to seek a sacrificial opportunity. He will have to search for it in the center, for it is there that the defender's main lines of communication meet.

PREVENTIVE (OR ANTI-CASTLING) SACRIFICES

All sacrifices which prevent the opponent from castling fall under this heading: their object is an early attack on the King.

In the planning of a game of chess, castling may well be said to be the most important move, as two pieces are developed at one stroke. The King, to be sure, does not get into play thereby, but making the King secure is at least the equivalent of a strong developing move. Communication between the Rooks is established or prepared for, and this in due course provides for the central development of all the forces.

We have frequently had occasion to observe the importance of this factor, especially in our study of obstructive sacrifices. There we have also seen how advantageous it is to attack with combined forces, and how detrimental to defend with scattered units. We have also learned that the most onerous obstructions are those which are lodged in the center. Viewed from this angle, it can easily be appreciated how valuable is the option of castling, and how great an advantage to debar the adversary from profiting by it. We have to assume, however, that the position is level in all other respects, and that nearly all the pieces are still on the board. As we get nearer to the endgame, the dangers to which the King is exposed become proportionately less. Also in closed games the loss of castling is of less moment, for the value of a tempo is not so great.

Castling is particularly important for the defending side. The first player, with his lead in development, is on the whole better able to forgo the privilege.

It is in most cases highly advantageous to prevent the opponent from castling. This therefore calls for willingness, when opportunity offers, to sacrifice material. The King, confined to his original square, not only hinders the development of his own forces; his position also facilitates the immediate launching of the hostile attack. This is particularly the case if one or even two center files are open.

In order to create such a desirable state of affairs, the attacker need not shrink from giving up a Pawn and at times even a piece.

The preventive sacrifice is more ambitious in its scope than the obstructive type, and therefore the stake can be greater in most cases.

Example 16

French Defense
Scheveningen, 1905

WHITE	BLACK	WHITE	BLACK
R. Spielmann	O. Duras	R. Spielmann	O. Duras
1 P-K4	P-K3	3 N-QB3	B-N5
2 P-Q4	P-Q4	4 B-Q3	PxP

4 ... P-QB4 is better. At that time the variation was quite unexplored.

5 BxP	N-KB3	8 PxP	BxNch
6 B-Q3	P-B4	9 PxB	Q-R4
7 P-QR3!	B-R4	10 N-K2	B-Q2

Better 10 ... QN-Q2.

11 O-O   QxP/B4?

A mistake. He should play 11 ... N-R3, as 12 BxN is not to be feared.

In this position White has the Bishop-pair and a slightly superior development. On the other hand, his Queen-side Pawns are weak. He must therefore avoid being drawn into a positional contest and seek open warfare. And so the chance of preventing his opponent's castling is most opportune. It looks as if this object could be achieved without a sacrifice. But appearances are deceptive. It soon becomes clear that in preventing Black from castling, White is called upon to show his willingness to give up material.

12 P-QR4!   B-B3

Not 12 . . . O-O?; 13 B-R3 etc.

13 B-R3   Q-KN4   14 P-B3!   . . . .

Much weaker, and even questionable, is 14 N-N3, or even 14 P-N3, after which Black can launch an attack with . . . P-KR4. The sacrificial idea underlying 12 P-QR4 now becomes apparent. This Pawn "hangs"—if 14 . . . BxRP; 15 B-B1?, Q-B4ch and Black is safe. Besides, the weakness at White's K3 invites a counterattack and necessitates the sacrifice of another Pawn.

14   . . . .   N-Q4   15 N-N3!   . . . .

The attack cannot be prepared in any other way. If for instance 15 Q-B1, QxQ—or 15 B-B1, N-K6—Black obtains the advantage.

15   . . . .   Q-K6ch

15 . . . NxP permits White to get a very strong attack with 16 Q-K1, NxP; 17 N-K4, BxN; 18 QxB, N-B4; 19 B-N5ch, QN-Q2; 20 Q-Q4.

15 . . . N-K6? would be entirely wrong, by the way, because of 16 Q-B1 threatening above all 17 P-KB4.

16 R-B2!   . . . .

And not 16 K-R1?, NxP! and Black forces the exchange of Queens.

16   ....   NxP   17   Q-KB1   ....

This square had to be vacated for the Queen.

17   ....   K-Q1

Black has to forgo castling on the other side as well.
18 N-B5! was too strong a threat, and the text move is as good
a parry as any.

18   B-N2   ....

The Bishop has fulfilled its purpose at R3. The attack proper
begins.

18   ....   N-Q4

Or 18 ... NxP; 19 BxNP, R-N1; 20 B-B6ch etc.

19   R-Q1   ....

19 BxNP was also advantageous. But in view of the exposed
position of Black's King, the first player is justified in going
after the major prize.

19   ....   N-Q2

Capturing the Rook Pawn is obviously too hazardous; there
follows 20 B-K4 and 21 P-QB4.

| 20 | B-K4 | Q-N3 | 21 | B-Q4 | Q-R4 |
| | | | 22 | P-QB4 | N/Q4-N3 |

[*See diagram on page 73.*]

23   Q-Q3!   ....

And not 23 BxB, PxB; 24 BxNch because of 24 ... PxB!
(24 ... QxB?; 25 Q-Q3!); 25 KR-Q2, R-R2 with good prospects for Black.

But now White threatens 24 BxB and 25 BxNch etc.

23 . . . . K-B1 24 R-N2! . . . .

The Rook is effectively posted here, as Black's Queen Knight Pawn is weak despite all possible cover and obstruction.

24 . . . . N-K4 25 Q-K2! . . . .

Petty would be 25 BxN/K5 etc. It is a curious circumstance that White offers to give up all his Queen-side Pawns with the sole object of denying the opposing King any rest.

25 . . . . N/K4xP

Black has no option. The Pawn was too strongly placed and, moreover, threatened to advance. But now White obtains a new base of operations in the Queen Bishop file.

26 R-B2 Q-N5

On 26 . . . QxP there follows 27 BxB, PxB; 28 R/Q1-QB1, N-R4; 29 Q-R6ch, K-Q2; 30 BxP, KR-KN1; 31 N-K4 and White's attack is irresistible (if 31 . . . K-K2; 32 B-B3).

27 R/Q1-QB1 N-R6

Or 27 . . . N-R4; 28 B-QB5!, Q-N6; 29 R-N2, QxRP; 30 R-R2 and White wins a piece.

28 RxBch! . . . .

Conclusive—a sacrifice for gain.

28	. . . .	PxR	29	RxPch	K-Q2
			30	B-QB5	Q-B5

The Knight cannot be saved. On other replies, 31 R-Q6ch decides the issue even more quickly.

31	Q-Q2ch	N-Q4	33	QBxN	R-Q1
32	R-Q6ch	K-K1	34	N-B5!	Q-B2

Or 34 . . . PxN; 35 RxRch, KxR; 36 BxN etc.

35	NxPch	K-B1	36	RxR dbl ch	KxN
			37	Q-N5 mate	

EXAMPLE 17

Queen's Gambit Declined
Match, 1910

WHITE	BLACK	WHITE	BLACK
R. Spielmann	J. Mieses	R. Spielmann	J. Mieses
1 P-Q4	P-Q4	5 N-B3	P-B3
2 P-QB4	P-K3	6 P-K3	Q-R4
3 N-QB3	N-KB3	7 N-Q2	B-N5
4 B-N5	QN-Q2	8 Q-B2	PxP

Still regarded by many as the best continuation.

9 BxN	NxB	10 NxP	Q-B2
		11 B-Q3	B-Q2

Poorly timed. Better was 11 . . . O-O or 11 . . . P-B4.

	12 P-QR3	B-Q3?

Quite bad. 12 . . . B-K2 had to be played.

13 P-K4   P-K4

The mistake on the previous move can hardly be rectified.
13 . . . B-K2 is answered by 14 P-K5 and 15 N-K4.

Black has committed the basic error of engaging an action
in the center before castling—an action which requires the
greatest circumspection, especially when on the defensive.
Here White is enabled to undertake a forceful preventive
combination. As in the previous game, its sacrificial character
will only be evident at a later stage.

14 P-B4!   . . . .

Threatens to win a piece and thus forces Black's reply.

14 . . . .   PxQP   15 P-K5   B-KB1

15 . . . PxN is answered by 16 NxBch and White has
achieved his purpose in preventing Black's castling.

16 PxN   PxN   17 Q-K2ch   . . . .

Now Black must renounce castling after all, 17 . . . B-K3
being refuted by 18 P-B5 etc.

17 . . . .   K-Q1   18 O-O-O!   . . . .

The point of the combination. Only by sacrificing the King Bishop Pawn does the attack gain sufficient momentum. 18 O-O, B-B4ch followed by . . . PxNP is not particularly troublesome for Black.

| 18 | . . . . | QxPch | 19 | K-N1 | K-B2 |

Black dare not capture at once at KB3 without getting into fatal difficulties: 19 . . . QxBP; 20 KR-B1, Q-K3 (else 21 B-B5); 21 N-K5 and wins.

| 20 | KR-B1 | Q-N4 | 21 | P-KR4! | . . . . |

Black cannot take this Pawn because of 22 Q-K5ch, K-B1; 23 B-B5! (much stronger than PxNP), which is immediately decisive.

Let us pause a little and try to classify this sacrifice. It is passive, as it can be declined by the opponent without disadvantage or without his position becoming worse; it is a sham sacrifice, as, strictly speaking, nothing is given up and something is to be gained; and it belongs to the category of mating sacrifices as its acceptance spells immediate destruction.

| 21 | . . . . | Q-QB4 | 23 | RxP | B-Q5 |
| 22 | PxNP | BxP | 24 | RxBch! | . . . . |

A decisive sacrifice for gain. Apart from the fact that it wins two pieces for the Rook, it also maintains the attack.

| 24 | . . . . | KxR | 25 | Q-N4ch | K-B2 |

Forced. If 25 . . . K-Q1 White wins with 26 B-B2 or 26 B-B5. If the King moves to the King file, there follows 26 Q-K4ch, K-B2; 27 R-B1ch, B-B3; 28 N-K5ch winning the Queen or mating in a few moves.

| 26 | Q-B4ch! | B-K4 |

Again forced. If the King moves to the Queen file, 26 B-B2 is decisive; and if 25 . . . K-B1; 26 B-B5ch follows.

27 NxB

Capturing with the Queen also wins. In my opinion, the attacker should not exchange Queens, or permit liquidation, as long as opportunities of attack remain; otherwise he gives up at least part of his advantage.

| 27 . . . . | QR-KB1 | 28 Q-R2! | Q-B7 |
| | | 29 B-B2 | . . . . |

29 . . . .   KR-N1

If 29 . . . Q-B5; 30 R-Q7ch and White wins as follows: (a) 30 . . . K-N1; 31 R-Q8ch followed by the exchange of Queens and 33 RxR; (b) 30 . . . K-B1; 31 Q-R3, K-N1; 32 RxPch, KxR (if 32 . . . K-R1; 33 RxPch); 33 Q-Q7ch and mate in a few moves; (c) 30 . . . K-N3; 31 N-B4ch! winning as in the game.

30 R-Q7ch   . . . .

With 30 N-N6 dis ch, K-N3 (the only chance); 31 NxR White maintains his extra piece as the counterattack 31 . . . RxP fails against 32 N-Q7ch, K-R3; 33 B-Q3ch, P-N4; 34

BxPch! followed by the victorious intervention of the White Queen.

The continuation adopted is based on the sacrifice of a piece and is even stronger.

30 ....   K-N3

Or 30 . . . K-B1; 31 Q-R3, K-N1; 32 RxPch! etc.

31 N-B4ch   K-R3

If 31 . . . K-N4; 32 Q-K5ch etc.

32 Q-B7!   ....

A precisely calculated mating sacrifice.

32 ....   Q-B8ch   33 K-R2!   ....

But not 33 R-Q1?, QxN; 34 B-Q3, P-B7ch! and Black wins.

33 ....   QxNch   36 B-Q3ch   K-R4
34 P-N3   Q-N4   37 Q-K5ch   P-B4
35 P-R4   Q-N3   38 RxNP!   ....

The point; so to speak, mating sacrifice, part two.

38 ....   RxPch   39 K-R3   R-N5

With 39 . . . P-B7 Black can play for this trap: 40
Q-K1ch?, Q-N5ch; 41 RxQ, P-B8(Q)ch; 42 QxQ, PxR mate!
But after 40 BxBP! the dream dissolves, as mate or loss of
the Rook cannot be avoided: 40 . . . RxB; 41 RxQ, PxR; 42
Q-K7, R-QR1; 43 Q-QN7, R-R3; 44 Q-B6 etc.

40 RxQ   PxR   41 Q-B7   Resigns

For 41 . . . R-QR1 is met by 42 Q-B6.

This and the preceding game present fairly simple forms
of the preventive sacrifice. In both cases, the stake was only
a Pawn. The evil of having to forgo castling in an open
position showed itself very clearly. The attack against the exposed King, with the defending forces partly undeveloped,
partly scattered, was easy to carry out, and opportunities for
various further sacrificial combinations occurred of themselves. Such attacks must be conducted without a let-up. It
does not do to be timorous or small-minded! One single tempo
can alter the whole situation. If this point was important in
the two previous cases, in the next two it becomes a matter
of vital consequence.

EXAMPLE 18

Scotch Game
Match, 1910

WHITE	BLACK	WHITE	BLACK
J. Mieses	R. Spielmann	J. Mieses	R. Spielmann
1 P-K4	P-K4	3 P-Q4	PxP
2 N-KB3	N-QB3	4 NxP	B-B4
		5 B-K3	B-N3

Simple and sound, and avoiding many book variations.

| 6 | B-QB4 | P-Q3 | 7 | N-QB3 | N-B3 |
| | | | 8 | NxN | .... |

With the subsequent pin in view, which White appears however to have overrated.

| 8 | .... | PxN | 9 | B-KN5 | O-O |

Provocative. 9 . . . B-K3—or 9 . . . PKR3; 10 B-R4, B-K3 —is sounder.

| | 10 | Q-B3 | B-K3 |

The solid move is 10 . . . B-Q5.

| | 11 | B-Q3 | .... |

He can play 11 BxN, QxB; 12 QxQ, PxQ; 13 B-Q3. Black, who relied on his two Bishops, would then have an approximately even game—but no more.

| 11 | .... | B-Q5 | 12 | Q-N3 | R-N1 |
| | | | 13 | N-Q1 | N-R4! |

[If 13 . . . BxNP?; 16 QR-N1, B-Q5; 17 RxR!, QxR; 18 P-QB3! and wins as 18 . . . B-QB4? is refuted by 19 BxN, while 18 . . . B-K4 is answered by 19 P-KB4!]

| 14 | Q-R4 | B-B3! | 15 | BxB | NxB |
| | | | 16 | P-KB4 | .... |

Threatens 17 P-K5, but 16 O-O was preferable.

| | 16 | .... | P-B4 |

At a pinch, 16 . . . N-K1 was good enough. Black wants to induce 17 P-QN3, in order to continue 17 . . . N-N5 and 18 . . . Q-B3.

If now 17 P-K5, P-B5!—which is threatened as it is.

| | 17 | P-B4 | .... |

Now the game is fairly even. Black can parry the threat of 18 P-K5, either by 17 . . . N-N5 or by 17 . . . N-Q2 18 QxQ, KRxQ!; 19 P-B5, N-K4!).

But the fact that White has not yet castled and is backward with the development of his pieces, gives rise to a surprising preventive sacrifice.

17 . . . . P-Q4! 18 KPxP . . . .

If 18 BPxP the same reply follows. After 18 P-K5, N-K5; 19 QxQ, KRxQ; 20 PxP—or 20 BxN—White has the better Pawn formation but is still at a disadvantage because of Black's far superior development.

18 . . . . BxP!! 19 PxB . . . .

Declining the offer was out of the question, as Black has an incidental threat of 20 . . . BxNP.

19 . . . . QxP

The sacrifice can now be appraised. Black has a piece less (the doubled Pawn hardly counts as compensation), but his advantage in development has increased enormously through the opening-up of the two center files. As both the Bishop and the King Knight Pawn are attacked, White cannot castle and must waste another tempo—unless he plays for equalization with 20 BxPch and 21 O-O. It is, however, hardly to be expected that White should make no attempt at refutation, and so Black can count on the chances of a violent central attack on the hostile King.

These were the considerations which led to the sacrifice. Only unbounded faith in the position and in the undeviating principles of development gave birth to the idea, for a previous instance of such a breakthrough is unknown to me even today.

I told myself that White, despite his extra piece, would be compelled to defend himself for a long time against a local supremacy and that, in these circumstances, the gain of at least some Pawns could be counted on. The course of the game speaks for the correctness—certainly from a practical standpoint—of this assumption.

20	Q-N3	KR-K1ch	21	B-K2	QR-Q1
			22	N-B3	....

Apart from 22 . . . Q-Q7ch a decision was threatened by 22 . . . RxBch!; 23 KxR, Q-B5ch!; 24 K-K1, R-K1ch etc. 22 K-B1 was likewise not playable for the same reason

22	....	Q-Q7ch	23	K-B1	N-Q4!

Far more powerful than 23 . . . QxP. In such positions, Pawns should not be captured until they fall in your lap, so to speak. Nothing counts but the attack.

24	R-K1	NxP	25	Q-B2	R-Q5
			26	P-KN3	....

The tempting 26 R-Q1 is demolished by the powerful reply 26 . . . QxBch! winning back the piece (27 QxQ, NxQ; 28 R-K1?, R-B5 mate!).

26	....	N-R6	27	Q-B5	....

27 Q-N2 leads to similar variations.

27   . . . .   QxP

28   QxN?   . . . .

He should play 28 N-Q1, although in that case Black also maintains good prospects after 28 . . . Q-Q7!; 29 QxN, R/Q5-K5; 30 N-B2! (best; 30 Q-N2?—or 30 Q-R5?, P-N3; 31 Q-B3—fails against . . . RxB! etc.), RxB; 31 RxR, QxRch; 32 K-N2, P-KR4! (32 . . . QxP?; 33 Q-Q7, Q-K3; 34 R-Q1 gives White the initiative). Now the second player has several strong threats: (a) continuation of the direct attack with . . . R-K3 or, if the hostile Queen moves away, first . . . P-R5; (b) march forward of the Queen Bishop Pawn; and (c) eventual gain of the fourth Pawn.

28 N-Q1 cannot, therefore, be considered the "refutation" of the sacrifice. The move actually made leads to speedy defeat.

28   . . . .   QxN   29 Q-B5   R/Q5-K5!

The pin on the Bishop is now deadly, as it completely paralyzes White's game.

30   Q-B2   Q-Q7   31 R-KN1   . . . .

There is no defense against the terrible threat of . . . R/K5-K3-KB3.

31	. . . .	R/K5-K3	33	B-B3	RxRch
32	R-N2	R-KB3		Resigns	

This game may not be particularly valuable in itself, but I consider it very instructive from the sacrificial point of view. I can well remember that, in the course of play, I was myself surprised at the terrific impact of the preventive sacrifice. I had always assessed it highly, but not highly enough. A very rewarding experience. Chance willed it that I should have to wait nearly twenty-five years before putting this experience to practical use. But I saw my way the more easily to bring a similar preventive sacrifice in the following game.

EXAMPLE 19

Grünfeld Defense
Sopron, 1934

WHITE	BLACK	WHITE	BLACK
E. Gereben	R. Spielmann	E. Gereben	R. Spielmann
1 P-Q4	N-KB3	4 P-K3	B-N2
2 P-QB4	P-KN3	5 N-B3	O-O
3 N-QB3	P-Q4	6 B-Q2	P-B3
		7 Q-N3	P-N3

Probably better than the usual continuation . . . PxP.

| 8 PxP | PxP | 9 R-B1 | . . . . |

Simpler 9 B-K2 and 10 O-O.

| 9 . . . . | B-N2 | 10 N-K5! | . . . . |

A sound idea.

10 .... KN-Q2 11 NxN? ....

Gives away two tempi. Logical is 11 P-B4, and if 11 . . . NxN; 12 BPxN, P-B3; 13 P-K6!; the advanced Pawn remains powerful. The text move leads to surprising turns.

White's last move looks unnatural. But how can it be answered? If Black replies 11 . . . QxN—apparently forced— White plays 12 B-N5 and 13 O-O, wins back the two tempi and has a good game. Yet there must be a way for Black to take advantage of his opponent's loss of time.

Is 11 . . . QxN really forced? As Black has gained two tempi, it is not far-fetched for him to think of giving up his Queen Pawn in order to gain still more tempi. We know that in open positions, three tempi are approximately worth a Pawn. Therefore:

11 .... NxN!

A sacrifice for development. Now if 12 NxP, P-K3; 13 N-B3, P-K4! White must either give back the Pawn or, by holding on to it, risk further very heavy loss of time.

The sacrifice for development has, however, still another trend. If White declines it with an indifferent move, there follows the opening-up of the center with . . . P-K4, which is in

Black's favor. And so I could foresee White's next move, for either acceptance of the sacrifice, or its refusal by an indifferent move, is too dangerous for White. And this was the basis of the subsequent sacrifice which was already under consideration when I played 11 . . . NxN.

12   P-B4   . . . .

A defensive Pawn-move, when his development is backward—that means the loss of another tempo. Black has already gained three tempi. This advantage, it is true, cannot be utilized in what is at present a close position. The following preventive sacrifice, however, opens up all lines at one stroke.

12   . . . .   P-K4!

Naturally 12 . . . N-B3 can also be played. The position is then equalized, for White can easily make up for the time lost. The fact, though, that White could give away three tempi without suffering thereby, would be a little humiliating for Black.

It is clear that White must take the proffered Pawn.

13   BPxP   NxP!

This is the idea behind the Pawn sacrifice! Note the striking similarity with the course of events in the preceding game. First of all, in both cases, a violent breakthrough by a Pawn against a seemingly bomb-proof point (here White's K5, there his Q5), and the sacrifice of a piece. In the present game we have a refinement in the developing sacrifice which served as a preamble. It is significant that the course of both games is cast in the same mold. The object of holding the King in the center and attacking him with all available forces is attained in both cases.

To decline the sacrifice in the present instance would be pointless, if only on positional grounds: 14 B-K2, N-B5! etc.

14 PxN   P-Q5!

The opening-up of lines must be carried out ruthlessly. In annotating this game for a chess periodical, I wrote the following comment at this stage: "The sacrifice of the Knight cannot be vindicated by analysis, and it would possibly have been refuted in a correspondence game. But in a contest over the board and with a time limit of eighteen moves an hour, it would nearly always win through."

That is the practical standpoint frequently upheld in this book.

If each and every sacrifice had to be of that cast-iron soundness which can be verified by analysis, it would be necessary to banish from the game of chess that proud and indispensable prerogative of the fighter: enterprise. All real sacrifices would have to disappear; only the sham sacrifices, which are in effect not sacrifices at all, would be allowed to remain.

15 N-Q1   . . . .

The sacrifice scores its first success: White is obviously afraid of the Queen check at KR5, and does not risk capturing the Queen Pawn. As matters stand, this check would not be the best continuation, because White would play K-Q1-B2, threatening a successful flight with his King. Black's best would be 15 . . . QxP, but in any event 15 PxP is White's best chance.

15	....	BxKP	16	P-K4	....

In order to close at least one of the center files. But this costs a Pawn, so that Black will already have two Pawns for his piece, and his attack remains just as strong.

16	....	BxKP	17	N-B2	B-Q4
			18	Q-KR3	....

White guards his King Knight Pawn in order to be able to develop his King Bishop. But already a third Pawn "hangs."

18	....	Q-K2

Naturally much stronger than capturing the Queen Rook Pawn.

19	B-K2?	....

The decisive mistake! White wants to castle in answer to 19 . . . BxQRP, when he actually gets a good game. But this intention is frustrated in deadly fashion, and Black's attack becomes irresistible.

The best defense, comparatively speaking, is 19 K-Q1 and if 20 . . . BxQRP; 21 B-QB4. It does not permanently cope with the danger, as Black still has three Pawns for the piece and White's King remains insecure; but at least White can make a real fight of it.

After the text move, White goes rapidly from bad to worse.

19	....	P-Q6!

A sweeping sacrifice for space. (See the following section on vacating sacrifices.)

The point is that after 20 NxP, KR-K1 White cannot castle, as Black's Q5 is now cleared for the Bishop, and so there follows 21 . . . B-Q5ch winning a piece and the game.

20 NxP   KR-K1   21 K-B1   . . . .

A difficult decision. Still more dangerous is 21 K-Q1, as the vacating sacrifice has opened the Queen file as well.

21   . . . .   BxQNP!

Recovery of the piece was already possible here by 21 . . . B-QB6; 22 BxB (obviously forced), QxBch; 23 K-N1, R-K6; 24 R-K1! RxQ; 25 RxQ, RxN. But White simply plays 26 P-QR3 and with Bishops of opposite color and only one Pawn less, he has excellent chances of a draw. The text move is far stronger:

22 R-K1   Q-B3ch   23 N-B2   . . . .

There is hardly anything else. If 23 N-B4 the Knight soon goes lost, and if 23 B-KB3, B-B5! wins.

23   . . . .   B-Q5   24 Q-KN3   R-K5!

Devastating! 24 . . . R-K4 is answered by 25 B-Q3. But now 25 B-Q3 is refuted by 25 . . . R-N5! etc.

25 P-KR4   . . . .

There is no adequate defense. After 25 Q-KB3 Black wins
by 25 . . . RxB!; 26 QxR, B-B5!; and if 25 B-KB3, B-B5ch;
26 K-N1, RxRch; 27 BxR, R-K1 and White's Bishop at K1 cannot be guarded, while if it moves, 28 . . . BxNch wins.

25   . . . .   QR-K1

Threatens 26 . . . RxB. White is powerless.

26 B-QN5   RxRch   27 BxR   R-K6!

Again there was an opportunity of regaining the piece and
this time with a winning position: 27 . . . RxBch; 28 KxR,
BxNch; 29 QxB, Q-R8ch; 30 K-Q2, QxR; 31 B-B1, Q-R7 etc.
But the continuation actually adopted winds up the game
much more rapidly.

28 Q-N5   . . . .

Or 28 Q-N8ch, K-N2; 29 B-N4, B-B4!; 30 BxB, Q-R8ch followed by mate in a few moves.

28	. . . .	RxBch	32	B-K2	B-B6!
29	KxR	QxNch	33	BxB	QxBch
30	K-Q1	BxNP	34	K-B2	BxR
31	R-K1	B-B6ch		Resigns	

The preventive sacrifice represents a sharply defined figure
in the world of combination. Only a few types can show such
singleness of purpose. It is in keeping with the character of
the preventive sacrifice that it is almost always active. In order
to achieve its highest aim, coercive pressure must be exerted
on the opponent.

Our four sacrifices are therefore all active sacrifices, even
that against Duras. For if in this game Black had renounced
the gain of a Pawn by 16 . . . NxP, White's attack would

have been much easier to conduct. In effect, acceptance was compulsory in this game also.

LINE-CLEARANCE SACRIFICES

The purpose of this type of sacrifice is to speed up the action of the major pieces, particularly that of the Rooks. It may be said to be an offshoot of the sacrifice for development.

The usual line-clearance sacrifice is passive: a Pawn is allowed to be captured in order to obtain an open file. The offer of the Knight Pawns is of frequent occurrence in this connection.

The active line-clearance sacrifice is intended to create a sudden superiority on a limited front by the unexpected participation of the major pieces.

In cases where the opponent has developed some serious weaknesses, although they may be screened in some way—by advanced Pawns, for example—this type of sacrifice can be very effective by tackling such weaknesses in brusque raiding style. It is a question of violently sweeping away the bastion behind which the enemy is about to marshal his forces.

At times the advantage gained by this type of sacrifice can be of paramount importance, especially where there is a possibility of a direct breakthrough against the King. Hence the clearance sacrifice frequently justifies the highest stakes.

EXAMPLE 20

Vienna Game
Mannheim, 1914

WHITE	BLACK	WHITE	BLACK
R. Spielmann	A. Flamberg	R. Spielmann	A. Flamberg
1 P-K4	P-K4	3 P-B4	P-Q4
2 N-QB3	N-KB3	4 BPxP	NxP
		5 N-B3	B-KN5

The best reply 5 . . . B-K2, which leads to an even game, had not yet been tried out when this game was played.

6 Q-K2   N-B4

Better 6 . . . NxN.

7 P-Q4   BxN?

And now 7 . . . N-K3 is preferable.

8 QxB   Q-R5ch?

8 . . . N-K3 is still comparatively best.

Evidently Black expects 9 Q-B2, whereupon the exchange of Queens will indeed assure him a perfectly satisfactory game. But the premature development of the Queen provides the first player with the opportunity for a powerful double clearance sacrifice.

9 P-N3!   QxQP   10 B-K3!   QxP

The acceptance of the first sacrifice was compulsory. The second could—and should—have been declined with 10 . . . Q-QN5. After 11 O-O-O, P-QB3 White would have a very good game, but not the much superior position which obtains here, where the open King file is of particular service to him.

11 O-O-O   ....

Now White has lost two Pawns, but he is greatly ahead in development, and, above all, he has the opportunity of bringing his Rooks speedily into action. The center Pawns, which are as a rule the most valuable, are nevertheless well suited, at the proper time, for a line-clearance sacrifice: the center files thus opened, allow the Rooks to get into play quickly and effectively.

11 ....   P-QB3

Black wishes to maintain his advantage in material at least, as consolation for his lack of development, but now his position is soon demolished. However, no other move is any better.

12 NxP!   ....

Thanks to the Rooks being in readiness for the attack, White can already strike the decisive blow. There is no risk attached to the sacrifice, as it secures a clear advantage in any event. In the sense of our classification, it must be viewed as a sacrifice for gain.

12 ....   PxN   13 RxP   ...

13   ....   Q-K3?

This leads to speedy defeat. 13 . . . Q-K5 is also insufficient because of 14 B-N5ch! and 15 BxN. .

The attack has a harder task after 13 . . . Q-B2. White can then liquidate and remain with an extra Pawn after 14 B-N5ch, N-B3 (other moves lose very quickly); 15 BxN, BxB; 16 RxB, O-O; 17 BxN, QR-B1; 18 BxP, QxR; 19 BxR, RxB. But in view of White's terrific attacking set-up, this would be a rather scrawny outcome.

A much stronger reply to 13 . . . Q-B2 is 14 B-KB4! with the following continuations:

I. 14 . . . Q-N3; 15 BxN!, RxB; 16 Q-B4!, R-B1 (if 16 . . . R-Q1; 17 B-N5ch, QxB; 18 R-K1ch, B-K2; 19 RxBch, KxR; 20 Q-K5ch etc.); 17 B-N5ch!, QxB; 18 R-K1ch, B-K2; 19 RxBch! KxR; 20 Q-Q6ch, K-K1; 21 R-K5ch, N-K3; 22 RxQ.

II. 14 . . . Q-R4; 15 B-N5ch!, QxB (if 15 . . . N-B3; 16 R-K5ch!); 16 R-K1ch, B-K2; 17 RxBch, KxR; 18 Q-K3ch etc.

III. 14 . . . Q-B1; 15 BxN, RxB; 16 B-N5ch, K-K2; 17 R-K1ch, N-K3; 18 Q-R3ch, K-B3; 19 R-B1ch, K-N3; 20 Q-Q3ch, K-R3; 21 Q-K3ch, P-N4; 22 RxNP!, NxR; 23 R-B6ch etc.

In all these variations, White wins easily. Therefore Black, in Variations I and III, has to refrain from recapturing after BxN, playing . . . B-K2 instead. In that case the first player, with equal material, still has a violent attack, the outcome of which is not in doubt.

Again we see that the continuation of the attack is preferable to a small gain in material.

14   B-QB4   ....

The principal threat is 15 RxN. Black no longer has a defense.

14   ....   Q-K5

Other moves also lose. The text move leads to an effective finish.

15 BxN   Resigns

One of those pleasing, if obvious, turns which mostly occur of themselves in won positions! Such a position hardly deserves a diagram, nor does the move rate an exclamation mark or comments such as "a brilliant Queen sacrifice." In our sense, it is merely a primitive mating sacrifice, which only requires calculating two moves ahead. After 15 . . . QxQ or 15 . . . QxB, only one glance suffices to perceive a forced mate by 16 R-K1ch etc.

From an artistic point of view, the previous line-clearance sacrifice of two Pawns is of greater value than the "sacrifice" of the Queen.

EXAMPLE 21

Allgaier Gambit
Munich, 1903

WHITE	BLACK	WHITE	BLACK
R. Spielmann	M. Eljaschoff	R. Spielmann	M. Eljaschoff
1 P-K4	P-K4	4 P-KR4	P-N5
2 P-KB4	PxP	5 N-N5	P-KR3
3 N-KB3	P-KN4	6 NxP	. . . .

The Knight sacrifice in the Allgaier Gambit, as far as this book is concerned, is a sacrifice for development.

6	KxN	8 BxPch	K-N2
7 B-B4ch	P-Q4	9 P-Q4	Q-B3

The usual move in those days was 9 . . . N-KB3 followed by 9 N-B3, B-N5. The text move originated in a consultation game at the Charkov Chess Club.

10	P-K5	Q-N3	13	O-O	P-B6
11	P-R5	Q-B4	14	N-K4	QxRP
12	N-B3	B-N5	15	N-N3	Q-R5

White is far better developed. True, he has himself only a few pieces in play, but compared with Black, he is a hundred percent better off! The second player's King, Queen, and King Bishop are all very badly placed; it were better had they not moved at all! White is in need of only one factor for victory: *the opening of a line* for his major pieces. The quicker he succeeds in obtaining it the more shattering the effect. To achieve this purpose, even a major sacrifice is justified. And in fact such a combination is available here:

16 RxP!   . . . .

As this move threatens destruction by 17 R-B7ch, acceptance of the sacrifice is compulsory.

16 . . . .   PxR   17 QxP   . . . .

White is now a Rook and Knight down. But the effect of the open King Bishop file is so overwhelming that Black must immediately give back a Knight.

17 . . . .   N-KB3

White threatened 18 Q-B7 mate. This point can only be

guarded by artificial interposition, for if 17 . . . Q-K2?;
18 N-R5ch followed by mate in two.

18 PxNch   K-B1

Again forced, for 18 . . . QxP?; 19 N-R5ch—or 18 . . . K-
N3; 19 Q-Q3ch, KxP; 20 B-KB4!—Black loses at once. Now the
King Bishop file is blocked, but in return the King file is open
and the advanced King Bishop Pawn cooperates very effectively.

There is now no immediately decisive continuation for
White. But his ability to bring all his pieces, particularly
Queen and Rook into play on the most advanced front, will
automatically bring a superabundance of threats, which Black,
in view of his meager development, will be unable to withstand for long or without heavy counter-sacrifices.

19 B-KB4!   . . . .

In the consultation game at Charkov, previously mentioned,
White played 19 B-K3 and won. In the Vienna Gambit Tournament played shortly before the present game, the same position occurred between Marco and Schlechter. Marco also
played 19 B-K3, but this move was finely refuted by Schlechter, namely by 19 . . . B-Q3; 20 N-B5, B-R7ch!—White's King
has to move to the King Bishop file, after which the King

Bishop Pawn can be captured without danger, and the advantage of a clear Rook decides the issue.

Luckily, perhaps, for me, I did not know either game, and therefore, confidently and without hesitation, I played 19 B-KB4! with the idea of 20 Q-K4 and the double threat of B-Q6ch and Q-N6.

19 . . . . N-R3

Black has no satisfactory move. If 19 . . . QxP; 20 B-Q6ch, K-N2; 21 N-R5ch etc. 19 . . . B-Q3 is also insufficient because of 20 BxBch, PxB; 21 Q-K3, R-R2; 22 R-K1, B-Q2; 23 BxP etc.

20 Q-K4! Q-N5

This appears to parry the two threats of 21 B-Q6ch and 21 Q-N6.

21 BxNP! . . . .

Decisive. If the Bishop is captured, Black's Queen is unguarded and goes lost by discovered attack (22 B-Q6ch or 22 BxPch). If Black does not effect the capture, he loses at least a piece.

Instead of the text move, 21 P-B3 is tempting, as the Bishop which is needed to protect Black's K2, has no move. But after 21 . . . B-Q2; 22 PxB, R-K1 Black can at least hold out longer than in the actual game.

21 . . . . BxB

Comparatively best. If he safeguards the Rook by 21 . . . QR-N1, White plays 22 BxN. Then 22 . . . BxB is out of the question, and apart from the attack White has three Pawns for the exchange—a decisive advantage in material.

22 BxPch RxB 23 QxQ R-R2

If 23 . . . RxP; 24 N-B5, R-B2; 25 Q-R5! (25 . . . K-K1; 26 N-R6 etc.).

24	Q-N6	R-B2	25	P-B3	B-Q3
			26	N-B5	....

Threatens 27 N-R6! The following counter serves only to postpone the execution of this threat.

26	....	B-K5	27	Q-R6ch	K-N1
			28	Q-N5ch	K-B1

If 28 . . . K-R2; 29 Q-R4ch etc.

29	N-R6	Resigns

EXAMPLE 22

King's Gambit

Teplitz-Schönau, 1922

WHITE	BLACK	WHITE	BLACK
R. Spielmann	E. Grünfeld	R. Spielmann	E. Grünfeld
1 P-K4	P-K4	6 P-Q4	B-N2
2 P-KB4	PxP	7 P-B3	P-KR3
3 B-B4	N-QB3	8 P-KN3	P-N5
4 N-KB3	P-KN4	9 N-R4	P-B6
5 O-O	P-Q3	10 N-Q2	B-B3

11   QNxP   . . . .

A typical line-clearance sacrifice, which we need not examine closely here, as it is well-known to the opening theorists.

11   . . . .   PxN   12   QxP   R-R2?

The correct defense is 12 . . . B-R6 followed by 13 . . . Q-Q2.

13   N-N6!   . . . .

Beginning a series of Knight maneuvers which will be painful for Black.

13   . . . .   R-N2   14   N-B4   . . . .

Threatens 15 N-R5.

14   . . . .   B-N5   15   Q-N2   B-N4
                              16   P-KR3   B-Q2

If 16 . . . BxN not 17 NPxB? because of 17 . . . Q-R5!, but 17 BxB, B-Q2; 18 QR-K1 with a powerful attack.

17   N-R5   R-R2

Black is a piece to the good, but his development is defective, his King-side menaced.

It is important to exploit this state of affairs before Black finds an opportunity to castle. This will be achieved by yet another line-clearance sacrifice.

18   P-K5!   . . . .

A preparatory vacating sacrifice. The White Queen needs the square K4.

18   . . . .   PxP   19   Q-K4   . . . .

Now the Rook is attacked, and, as the protection of Black's KB2 must be maintained, Black's reply is forced.

19 . . . .   P-B4

20 RxP!   . . . .

This was what White was planning! White will be a whole Rook down, but all doors and gates will be opened for his remaining forces. A striking feature is the fact that White can embark on this sacrifice with his Queen-side undeveloped. But it is often preferable not to develop a piece at all than to place it on an indifferent square. In the present case, the King Bishop file is opened completely, and will soon be occupied by the other White Rook for immediate and decisive action. The pioneer at KB1 had to pave the way for the cannon now at QR1. We saw the same procedure in the preceding game.

20 . . . .   BxR

To 20 . . . BxB the simplest reply is 21 RxB.

21 QxB   . . . .

Now the Black position is so broken up that the White forces, in their coming assault, will have no serious obstacles to overcome. There are already divers threats, so that Black will be unable to conserve his material.

21 .... R-K2

Or 21 . . . Q-Q2; 22 B-K6 and 23 BxN etc.

22 BxB PxB 23 R-KB1! ....

He can play 23 BxN at once, but the text move threatens 24 B-B7ch and mate in a few moves. Black must pay heavily in order to hold out a little longer.

23 .... Q-Q3

Or 23 . . . N-R3; 24 N-B6ch, K-B1; 25 QxNP etc.

24 BxN PxP

Desperation. After 24 . . . K-Q1 the game is also lost.

25 Q-B8ch K-Q2 26 QxR ....

Now it is White who has the extra piece! The rest is silence.

26	....	Q-B4	29	K-N2	P-Q6
27	N-B6ch	K-Q3	30	R-B2	Q-K8
28	Q-KB8	Q-K4	31	Q-R6	Resigns

In the two preceding games the attacker, it is true, made considerable sacrifices in material; yet he won quickly. For all that, it would be unjust to classify them as sham sacrifices.

Whoever invests a whole Rook in a "deal" must, in the nature of things, feel satisfied that it is going to "pay." It would happen but seldom for anyone to sacrifice a whole Rook, without having strong and immediate threats at his disposal. In the whole of chess literature, I know of only one such case, the game Maroczy-Tartakover (Teplitz-Schönau, 1922)—a masterpiece of Tartakover's.

After a Rook sacrifice, the defender as a rule has many opportunities for counter-sacrifice. Herein lies the essential difference between Rook sacrifices and those involving less material. For this reason, Rook sacrifices are much more difficult to probe. A thorough scrutiny of all possible variations is hardly practicable under a time limit. Hence the attacker must rely largely on intuition.

Only such Rook sacrifices must be classed as sham, which bring about a decision after a few checks or other forced continuations.

VACATING SACRIFICES

The object of a vacating sacrifice is to clear a certain square for a certain piece. It is therefore sharply defined.

As with all other types, we have here both sham and real sacrifices.

In the case of sham vacating sacrifices, the stake is not limited, as the material given up will be recovered or a mate brought about. Not so with the real vacating sacrifice. As the only object in view is to place one individual piece on a better square, that is, increase its effectiveness, and as there is no possibility of bringing about an immediate decision thereby, it is practically out of the question to incur large risks in material.

The transaction can hardly justify a charge of more than one or two Pawns, usually only one.

As we have had occasion to note before, the collaboration of two or more types of sacrifices occurs occasionally. Very often in such instances the vacating sacrifice is the precursor. A certain square must be made available for a certain piece, and only then can the combination proper set in. Such a case may be seen in Example 22.

As a self-contained maneuver, that is, without being followed up by further sacrifices, the genuine vacating sacrifice is of less frequent occurrence. For all that, it is not less important than other types. At times the weal or woe of an attack, and with it of a game, depends on the action of one single piece; if it is effective, it helps other pieces to put forth their maximum effect; let it fall short, and the power of the whole army is paralyzed. The ultimate result may then easily depend on a vacating sacrifice.

EXAMPLE 23

Giuoco Piano

Carlsbad, 1907

WHITE	BLACK	WHITE	BLACK
R. Spielmann	D. Janowski	R. Spielmann	D. Janowski
1 P-K4	P-K4	3 B-B4	B-B4
2 N-KB3	N-QB3	4 P-B3	P-Q3

The Möller Attack was feared in those days. To avoid it, however, it is better to play 4 . . . B-N3 or 4 . . . Q-K2.

5 P-Q4	PxP	6 PxP	B-N3
		7 P-KR3	....

Else 7 . . . B-N5 is annoying.

7	N-B3	8 O-O	....

On 8 N-B3 the following move is disagreeable.

8	NxKP

After 8 . . . O-O; 9 R-K1 the same continuation could arise as in the actual game.

If Black forgoes the following liberating maneuver—a positional sacrifice—White obtains the advantage because of his powerful center.

9 R-K1	O-O

Or 9 . . . P-Q4; 10 BxP, QxB; 11 N-B3 etc.

10 RxN	P-Q4	11 B-KN5!	Q-Q3

Not 11 . . . P-B3; 12 B-N3, PxB; 13 N-B3 etc.

| 12 BxP | QxB | 13 N-B3 | Q-Q2 |

13 . . . Q-R4? will not do because of 14 P-Q5 followed by 15 B-K7 and 16 B-N4, winning.

| 14 P-Q5 | P-B3 |

Else White's Rook penetrates to K7.

| 15 B-K3! | N-Q1 |

The alternative 15 . . . N-K2 leads to similar play.

| 16 BxB | RPxB | 17 Q-K2 | N-B2 |
| | | 18 R-K7 | Q-Q1 |

The White Rook has penetrated to K7 after all, but Black threatens to trap it by . . . N-K4. It is clear that White's positional advantage will dwindle perceptibly if he has to withdraw the Rook. There is, however, a maneuver by which the Rook is firmly established on this excellent square.

19 P-Q6! . . . .

In this way the square Q5 becomes available for the Queen Knight, which can take a hand at once and support the Rook at K7. As a result, White not only maintains the favorable disposition of his pieces, but strengthens it very considerably. A typical vacating sacrifice!

19 ....   NxP

The only possible way. 19 . . . QxP fails because of 20 N-QN5, with 21 NxP to follow, and White regains his Pawn with a greatly improved position; again 19 . . . PxP is not feasible because after 20 N-Q5 followed by N-Q4, R-K1 and P-B4, Black's position would eventually become quite helpless.

20 N-Q5   R-B2

Here Black can dislodge the Rook, beginning with 20 . . . P-B3, but only at the cost of other ills. The continuation might be: 21 N-B4! (not 21 N-B7?, N-B4!), N-B4; 22 Q-B4ch, K-R1; 23 R-K4. Now White has a very strong position in which his control of the center files is particularly beneficial: the doubling of the Rooks is threatened as well as N-K6, whereas Black has difficulties with his development. Nor can he play 23 . . . N-Q3? because of 24 N-N6ch and 25 R-R4 mate.

21 R-K1   B-Q2

After 21 . . . RxR; 22 NxRch, K-B1; 23 Q-Q3!—or 22 . . . K-R1; 23 N-R4!—White has an excellent position.

Quite bad is 21 . . . RxP? because of 22 RxR, KxR (22 . . . NxR? allows mate by 23 Q-K8ch etc.); 23 Q-Q3 and there is no adequate defense against the treble threat of 24 Q-N3 or 24 QxP or 24 R-K7ch.

22 N-R4   R-R4

If 22 . . . RxP White continues as in the actual game.

23 RxR   NxR

Or 23 . . . KxR; 24 Q-R5ch, K-N1; 25 R-K7 with the decisive threat 26 NxPch.

24 N-B5!   . . . .

A remarkable position: both Knights are offered as sham sacrifices, and neither can be taken; one because of material loss, the other because of mate. The combination leads to a considerable strengthening of White's position.

24 . . . .   N-K4   25 N/B5-K7ch   K-R1
The same continuation follows after 25 . . . K-B1.

26 P-QN4!   R-R1   27 P-B4   N-N3

Or 27 . . . N-B3; 28 Q-R5, B-K1; 29 Q-N4 with a very violent attack (29 . . . B-Q2; 30 Q-R4 threatening 31 NxKBP). On 27 . . . N-B2; 28 Q-R5 is even stronger.

28 NxNch   PxN   29 N-K7   Q-K1

After 29 . . . B-K1 Black's KB1 is unprotected later on. White's attack is becoming irresistible.

                30 Q-KB2!   P-KN4

Compulsory.

31 PxP   PxP   32 Q-Q2!   P-N4

The King Knight Pawn cannot be saved. If 32 . . . P-N5; 33 Q-N5 is immediately decisive.

33	QxP	R-R3	34	R-K4	R-R3
			35	N-B5!	....

Wins at least the exchange.

35	....	Q-N3	36	Q-Q8ch	....

Not 36 NxR? QxR!

36	. .	K-R2	38	R-N4	R-N4
37	QxB	R-R4	39	R-R4ch	Resigns

The effects of a well-timed vacating sacrifice are seen here in the clearest light. At the critical moment, White has a good game and can maintain a satisfactory position by retiring his Rook. But he turns his favorable position to far better account by means of the Pawn sacrifice. It is instructive to observe how, as a consequence of the powerful position of the Knight at Q5, all the White pieces join very quickly in effectively concentrated action.

When it is a question of spurring on critically posted pieces to give of their best, a small sacrifice can often work wonders.

EXAMPLE 24

King's Gambit
Abbazia, 1912

WHITE	BLACK	WHITE	BLACK
R. Spielmann	R. Réti	R. Spielmann	R. Réti
1 P-K4	P-K4	3 N-KB3	N-KB3
2 P-KB4	PxP	4 N-B3	P-Q4
		5 P-K5	....

Better is 5 PxP; at the time this variation had not been explored very thoroughly.

| 5 .... | N-K5 | 6 B-K2 | N-QB3 |

Pointless. 6 ... B-QB4 and if 7 P-Q4, B-QN5! gives Black a favorable position as in a similar variation of the Vienna Game.

| 7 P-Q3 | NxN | 8 PxN | P-KN4 |
| | | 9 O-O | KR-N1 |

Beginning an ingenious if premature attack, which will ultimately be repelled conclusively. 9 ... B-K3—or 9 ... P-KR3—is in order.

| 10 P-Q4 | P-N5 |

10 ... B-K3 is still in order.

| 11 N-K1 | P-B6 | 12 B-Q3 | Q-R5 |
| | | 13 B-KB4 | PxP |

White was threatening 14 B-N3 followed by 15 PxP etc.

| 14 NxP | Q-R4 | 16 P-B4 | B-K3 |
| 15 R-N1! | N-Q1 | 17 N-K3 | PxP |

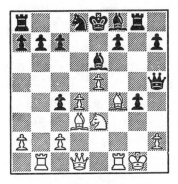

White's position is superior. Black's premature attack is at a standstill and has only damaged his own position, leaving him with insufficient development and a weakened King-side. As against this, the first player has mobilized his forces effectually and is now about to eliminate the barricades in the center. Once the center becomes fluid, the attack must pass over to White and swell mightily. But it must be followed up sharply, for otherwise Black might recuperate and even resume his own attack with renewed strength. The key to the' position is White's Q5. If he gains control here, his attack will flare up suddenly. The sooner this preliminary object is attained, the more likely the success.

With the last moves, the conquest of the critical square was begun and Black was forced to exchange at White's QB4. 17 . . . P-QB3 would only have led to further lines being opened, much to White's advantage: 17 . . . P-QB3; 18 PxP, PxP; 19 P-B4 etc. These explanations will make clear the idea underlying the next move.

18   B-K4!   . . . .

Much stronger than recapturing at QB4, which only diverts the White pieces from the attack on Q5: 18 NxBP?, B-Q4! and Black begins to threaten in turn—or 18 BxBP, BxB; 19 NxB, N-K3 and Black suddenly obtains counterchances: he threatens 20 . . . NxB followed by . . . Q-R6 and . . . P-N6. Theoretically White would still have the best of it, but in such wild positions practical chances count for more than theory.

The move in the text indicates that 16 P-B4 was not intended simply as an offer to exchange, but rather as a vacating sacrifice. There is now the powerful threat 19 P-Q5, which Black must prevent, or at least minimize, at all cost. We see now that 17 . . . PxP was at any rate better than 17 . . . P-QB3; for the following move is the only useful reply to White's threat.

18   . . . .   P-QB3   19   P-Q5!   . . . .

Logical play: the road to victory is via Q5. Tempting is the combination 19 RxP, NxR; 20 BxPch and 21 BxN, which yields

White an overwhelming attacking position—but for the flaw that Black is not obliged to capture the Rook: he interpolates 19 . . . B-R3, after which White may very likely find himself in trouble.

19 .... B-QB4

Again most ingenious, and again . . . inadequate. Obviously Réti shares my view that 19 . . . PxP; 20 NxQP, BxN (forced); 21 QxB gives White a won game.

20 K-R1! ....

Over-hasty is 20 PxB, for there follows 20 . . . NxP; 21 Q-K2, NxB; 22 RxN, QxP; 23 QR-KB1, P-N6 and suddenly Black has formidable counterplay: he has four extra Pawns and stands to recover his piece. It would therefore be in the highest degree illogical on the part of the first player to be drawn into complications for the sake of winning a piece. The plan of campaign was to obtain a strong attacking position by getting control of the point Q5, and the text move keeps this plan going in a consistent manner.

20 .... BxN

Still well aware that his position after 20 . . . PxP; 21 NxQP is untenable. Black now loses a piece, but operates for some time with a variety of dangerous threats. However, as White has the better development and in addition has an extra piece, victory in the end falls—logically—to the bigger battalions.

21	PxB!	NxP

The alternative 21 . . . BxB fails against 22 Q-Q7ch, K-B1; 23 RxB.

22	BxB	QxP	23	BxKRP!	R-R1

If 23 . . . R-N2; 24 B-B4! (24 . . . NxB?; 25 R-K1) with the attack and easily maintaining the extra material.

The text gives the impression that Black is about to regain the piece, as after 24 B-B4? Black has the powerful reply 24 . . . Q-R4!

24	RxBP!	....

Only this mating sacrifice finally puts an end to Black's dreams. If the Rook is taken, White wins by 25 Q-Q7ch followed by 26 R-B1ch etc. On the other hand, White threatens mate on Q7, so that Black's reply is practically forced.

24	....	R-Q1	25	QxP!	....

So as to win by 26 RxPch, if his Rook is taken.

25	....	QxB

At last he has recovered the piece, but . . .

26 B-N6!	Resigns

There is nothing to be done against the numerous threats of discovered check.

As in the preceding game, the vacating sacrifice indirectly brought about the decision. In each case the prime object was to help one single piece to carry out a special task, but the effect was that the attack gathered a sudden momentum. If the success was greater in the second example, the explanation is that the attacker at the time of the sacrifice had already gained a considerable advantage.

DEFLECTING OR DECOY SACRIFICES

Problem lovers are conversant with this sacrifice, but only in its sham form. In practical play we mostly find the real type in its passive form. This occurs in those cases of advanced development where attack and counterattack strive for mastery.

As a rule, the course of events runs as follows: each side advances on opposite wings. In the nature of things, the original attacker—generally the first player—has the edge, as his pieces should be positionally better placed for the attack. And so the opportunity frequently arises of thwarting the counterattack, not by defensive moves, but by ruthlessly pressing home one's own attack.

The roles are mostly so distributed that the original attack operates on the King-side and the counterattack on the Queen-side; this follows the normal trend of opening strategy. While the counterattack gains space and material on the Queen-side, the hostile threats accumulate on the King-side. Frequently the decision falls on the King-side before the defender can transfer his troops from their raid to cooperate in the defense.

A similar mode of procedure is often used in the opening stage. But here, if a counterattack is deliberately disregarded, it is done on general principles of development and not in deference to any particular attack. Therein lies the difference between the sacrifice for development and the decoy sacrifice: there the general purpose, here the single, definite object.

EXAMPLE 25

Giuoco Piano
(in effect)
Hamburg, 1910

WHITE	BLACK	WHITE	BLACK
R. Spielmann	L. Forgács	R. Spielmann	L. Forgács
1 P-K4	P-K4	3 B-B4	B-B4
2 N-KB3	N-QB3	4 P-QN4	B-N3
		5 P-B3	. . . .

A harmless continuation which leads into Bird's variation of the Giuoco Piano. More incisive is 5 P-QR4 or 5 B-N2. Generally speaking, the Evans Gambit Declined produces an even game.

5	N-B3	7 P-QR4	P-QR3
6 P-Q3	P-Q3	8 B-K3	BxB

8 . . . B-R2 is more prudent. 8 . . . N-K2 can also be considered, with the idea of bringing the Knight to KB5 via KN3, after 9 BxB, PxB.

9 PxB	P-Q4	11 BxN	QxB
10 PxP	NxQP	12 P-K4	Q-Q3
		13 O-O	O-O

Here 13 . . . B-K3 (with a view to . . . R-Q1) looks inviting. But White can forestall the threatened pressure on his Q3 with a promising Pawn sacrifice: 13 . . . B-K3; 14 P-Q4, PxP; 15 PxP, N (or Q)xNP; 16 N-R3 etc.

14 N-R3   R-Q1?

Weakens the King-side. He should develop the Bishop. Black plays for a combination which will be refuted by a counter-combination.

15 P-N5   Q-B4ch   16 K-R1!   ....

If 16 P-Q4?, KPxP! with advantage to Black.

16 . . . .   N-R4

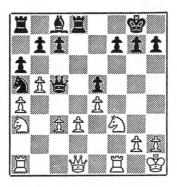

In pursuing his plans on the Queen file, Black has denuded his King of his protecting pieces. White seizes the opportunity to launch a sharp attack.

17 P-Q4!   ....

Instead of this 17 N-N5 is tempting, but Black simply answers 17 . . . P-KB3 and now there is no forcible continuation, as 18 Q-R5? fails because of 18 . . . PxN. Hence Black's Queen must first be diverted from the diagonal QR3-KB8.

17 . . . .   QxBP

The acceptance of the sacrifice is extremely hazardous. 17 . . . Q-K2 intending 18 NxP, P-KB3 winning back the Pawn by 19 . . . QxP is to be considered—or else 17 . . . PxP; 18 PxP, Q-R4. But with this line of play Black would admit that his counterattack has been ill-judged, and no player likes to make such an admission.

18 N-N5!   ....

Now that Black's Queen is out of the way, this move is very powerful.

18   ....   B-K3

If instead 18 . . . P-KB3; 19 Q-R5 and Black dare not take the Knight because of the resulting mate in three moves. But if he plays 19 . . . P-R3 the continuation is 20 Q-B7ch, K-R1; 21 Q-K7 and wins.

Also if Black captures the Queen Pawn instead of playing the text move, or plays 18 . . . R-B1, there follows 19 Q-R5, which in the first case decides at once; in the second, soon. The text move is therefore forced.

19   Q-R5   P-R3

20   P-Q5!   ....

Capturing on KB7 or K6 is appreciably weaker. The move in the text smashes Black's King-side.

20   ....   PxN

He has no choice.

21   PxB   PxKP   22   Q-B7ch   K-R2
                        23   QR-B1!   ....

The decoyed, badly posted Queen provides an opportunity

for a sacrifice for gain. Black has nothing better than taking the Knight.

23	....	QxN	24 RxP	Q-B1

Again forced. White wins the Queen for Rook and Knight, and still maintains the attack.

25 Q-R5ch	K-N1	26 RxQch	RxR
		27 P-R4!	....

Threatens 28 Q-N6, as well as 28 RPxP followed by 29 P-KN6.

27	....	QR-B1	28 P-N6!	....

Again threatening Q-N6.

28	....	RxR	29 PxR	R-B1
			30 Q-Q1	Resigns

This game is of no great value except as a suitable example of an active decoy sacrifice. It is in the nature of this type of sacrifice that the stake in material is rather small. Usually a Pawn, sometimes the exchange is given up. More substantia units can be sacrificed only in exceptional circumstances.

The decoy sacrifice occurs constantly in practical chess; the principles underlying it are, in the main, generally known. I have quoted it for the sake of completeness and can refrain from giving further examples.

(CASTLED) KING'S FIELD SACRIFICES

Among the various types of sacrifices, those in the King's Field claim the largest share of our attention. In this book, too, this fact will be taken into consideration.

Castling provides for the safeguarding of the King and, at the same time, for the development and coordination of the

Rooks. Castling is advantageous in itself. Those cases in which a player can afford not castling with most of the pieces still on the board, are definitely exceptional. If mistakes have been made in the course of a game, however, even the castled position may become fatal to the defender's King. Near the corner of the board the re-grouping of pieces, suddenly rendered necessary, can only be carried out with difficulty: there is little room and moreover, in the nature of things, assistance can only come from one direction.

Castling, a blessing when employed and exploited correctly, can become a curse in consequence of a mistake.

In King's Field sacrifices a piece is the usual stake. A Pawn is rarely given up, except in the course of a Pawn-storming attack. However, there are occasions when a single Pawn acts as a spearhead and immolates itself in order to make a breach in the castled position.

Under the name of King's Field sacrifice, we understand only such sacrifices as occur within reach of the hostile Pawns in the castled position, namely the Bishop, Knight and Rook Pawns. For instance, if the attacker gives up his own Pawn at KN2 in order to open the King Knight file and initiate a direct Kingside attack, this is in our sense a line-clearance sacrifice.

The object of denuding the hostile King and confining him to a corner, is a major purpose for which at times the heaviest sacrifices can be made.

Most of these are of course only transient: they bring about an immediate decision, and belong to the class of sham sacrifices.

Our attention will be confined to the *real* type of King's Field sacrifice.

EXAMPLE 26

French Defense
Bussum, 1934

WHITE	BLACK	WHITE	BLACK
R. Spielmann	Dekker	R. Spielmann	Dekker
1 P-K4	P-K3	2 P-Q4	P-Q4
		3 N-Q2	N-KB3

The continuation 3 . . . P-QB4 is accepted as best.

4 P-K5   . . . .

Good in this case, as the center can be supported easily.

4	KN-Q2	7 QN-B3	Q-N3
5 B-Q3	P-QB4	8 N-K2	PxP
6 P-QB3	N-QB3	9 PxP	B-N5ch
		10 K-B1!	. . . .

Very strong in this case, as the simplifying exchange desired
by Black is avoided. Artificial castling will be quite easy later
on for White. Aside from this, the move has a definite object.

10 . . . .   O-O?

Black was at a loss for a good move here. Development on the Queen-side was in the spirit of the position. But a solution of the problem was not easy to find—not, at any rate, without loss of time. A laborious but perhaps feasible course was 10 . . . Q-Q1 followed by 11 . . . N-N3 and 12 . . . B-Q2; the loss of time need not be fatal, given the closed nature of the position.

But 10 . . . O-O? is a decisive mistake. Any fairly experienced player knows that in this type of position castling on the King-side is dangerous if not downright bad. The reason is found in the Bishop sacrifice at KR7. This, the best-known of King's Field sacrifices, leads—where possible at all—mostly to a forced win. On general lines the scheme is 1 BxRPch, KxB; 2 N-N5ch, K-N1; 3 Q-R5 and a death-warrant through mate or exhaustion of Black's resources.

My opponent was fully aware of these considerations, nor was he thoughtless in castling. If he made a fatal blunder thereby, the reason lies in the conviction, inbred in the majority of chessplayers, that the Bishop sacrifice at KR7 can only be correct if it leads to an immediate win. It is commonly looked upon as a short mating combination rather than a real sacrifice. In *this* sense the Bishop sacrifice is not indicated in the diagram position. Viewed, however, as a real sacrifice, it unleashes a very violent attack and can be ventured without misgiving.

11	BxPch!	KxB	12	N-N5ch	K-N1

The only move. If 12 . . . K-N3?; 13 N-B4ch and mate in a few more moves.

13	Q-Q3!	. . . .

The point. The Queen could not reach the King Rook file according to the usual routine (Q-R5); the goal will be reached via Q3.

If now 13 . . . P-N3 or 13 . . . P-B4 there is already a win

by 14 Q-KR3, thus: 13 . . . P-B4; 14 Q-KR3, R-K1; 15 Q-R7ch, K-B1; 16 N-B4.

Hence Black must move his King Rook and White's Queen penetrates at once. This circumstance is already enough to justify the Bishop sacrifice: once the hostile King has been forced to flee, further attacking opportunities will turn up automatically. I feel that I must be most emphatic on this point. *The idea of calculating every sacrifice with the utmost exactitude is fundamentally wrong.* Faith in the position is required, and faith in oneself. A game of chess is not a mathematical problem, but a contest full of life, and in a contest, the attacker, in practice, always has the advantage.

| 13 | .... | R-K1 | 15 | Q-R8ch | K-K2 |
| 14 | Q-R7ch | K-B1 | 16 | QxP | K-Q1 |

After this, White wins a third Pawn, thus obtaining sufficient compensation for his piece.

Why did Black fail to protect his Bishop Pawn, which he could have done in one of two ways?

As I noticed that my opponent was reflecting for a long time, although the defense 16 . . . R-B1 seems so obvious, I went more deeply into the position and noticed that the reply 17 NxKP! wins at once (group: sham sacrifice; type: mating sacrifice), thus: 16 . . . R-B1; 17 NxKP!, KxN; 18 N-B4ch, K-B4 (if 18 . . . K-K2; 19 NxPch wins the Queen); 19 Q-R7ch followed by 20 Q-R5 mate. Or if 17 . . . R-K1, the menaced King is hounded to death: 18 B-N5ch, KxN; 19 N-B4ch, K-B4; 20 Q-R7ch, KxB; 21 N-R3ch, K-N5; 22 P-B3 mate.

When I saw that defending with the Rook (16 . . . R-B1) ends in failure, I also examined the unnatural-looking protect-·ing move 16 . . . N-Q1 and perceived immediately that this fails also, the continuation being 17 NxBP!, NxN; 18 B-N5ch and wins.

Note, by the way, that in both cases (16 . . . R-B1 and 16 . . . N-Q1), White could not solve the problem by trying to win the King Bishop by means of 17 P-QR3 etc. Besides being in principle a miserly move—it deviates from the main object— it would fail because Black has the resource 17 . . . Q-R3!

I was convinced, when playing 11 BxPch!, that the attack was bound to win out somehow. Yet it gave me great satisfaction to see the soundness of the sacrifice confirmed so soon and so conclusively.

17   QxP   . . . .

Not only winning a third Pawn, but revealing a new weakness (Black's King Pawn). Moreover, the Black King's last bulwark has fallen. The move is much stronger than capturing with the Knight, after which the King could continue his flight.

17 . . . . N-B1

Liquidation by 17 . . . NxQP is past hope: 18 B-K3, B-B4; 19 BxN, BxB; 20 NxB, QxN; 21 NxPch, RxN; 22 QxR.

If now (a) 22 . . . NxP; 23 Q-B6ch followed by 24 R-K1, or 24 R-B1ch and 25 R-K1; (b) 22 . . . QxKP; 23 QxQ, NxQ; 24 R-Q1 (24 . . . B-K3?; 25 R-K1!); and finally (c) 22 . . . QxNP; 23 R-K1—with an easy win for White in each case.

18 P-KR4! . . . .

Now this Pawn advances unhindered to queen.

18 . . . . B-Q2

At this stage, it is even worse to capture the Queen Pawn: 18 . . . NxQP?; 19 B-K3, B-B4; 20 R-B1 and there is no reply to the threat 21 RxB.

If 20 . . . NxN, White wins by 21 RxB! threatening 22 RxBch. 21 BxB leaves Black the resource 21 . . . Q-R3 (which cannot be played after 21 RxB! because of the mate threatened on B7).

19	B-K3	R-B1	22	P-R6	NxBch
20	P-R5	N-K2	23	PxN	B-N4ch
21	N-B4	N-B4	24	K-N1	R-B2
			25	P-R7	. . . .

With this sham sacrifice of the Queen, White wins a Rook.

25 . . . . RxQ

If 25 . . . NxP; 26 N/N5xPch is conclusive.

26 NxRch K-Q2

Or 26 . . . K-K2; 27 P-R8(Q), KxN?; 28 Q-B6ch, K-N1; 29 R-R8 mate.

27	P-R8(Q)	N-N3	29	QxN	B-Q6
28	Q-B6	NxN	30	R-R8	B-B1

| 31 | N-Q6 | BxN | 33 | PxB | QxNP |
| 32 | RxR | KxR | 34 | Q-B6! | .... |

Another "sacrifice"!

34	....	QxRch	37	Q-B7ch	K-N4
35	K-R2	K-Q2	38	P-Q7	Q-Q8
36	Q-K7ch	K-B3	39	QxPch	Resigns

If 39 . . . K-R5 (or 39 . . . K-B5); 40 Q-N3ch and the Pawn queens.

In this example, the sacrificial attack won through without much difficulty, but the essence of the "real" sacrifice was preserved. At the critical point, it was clear only that White stood to gain two Pawns for his piece, while he maintained the attack. Whether the attack was to succeed, had to be left to positional judgment. It was no mere accident that the gain of a third Pawn, with unabated attack, followed immediately.

In certain circumstances, especially with ample time on the clock, it might have been possible to calculate the consequences of the sacrifice up to a clear win. Had I done so, I should have called this method faulty! Occasionally this procedure may lead to success, but it would be exceptional.

How difficult it is at times to see correctly a few moves ahead with their variations, and how often has such a useless waste of energy led to nervous exhaustion, time difficulties and entirely unnecessary losses!

If I claim some credit in this particular game for having gauged the sacrifice correctly, it is done in no boasting spirit. On the contrary: intuitive play, unfortunately, is not rated very highly. Many chessplayers, even not a few masters, are loath to admit subsequently that at a critical point they were guided by instinct; some have been known to demonstrate how amazingly far ahead and accurately they have made their calculations. This strikes me as petty rather than heroic. Exact calculation is, generally speaking, needed more in defensive positions than in attack, and is, of course, essential in sham sacrifices. The expert chessplayer must be good at analysis, but he must not overdo it.

This disquisition obviously refers only to match or tournament play with a time limit averaging three-four minutes per move. An entirely different perspective obtains in postal chess. Here it is more easily possible to seek ultimate truths.

EXAMPLE 27

Danish Gambit Declined
(in effect)
Nuremberg, 1906

WHITE	BLACK	WHITE	BLACK
P. S. Leonhardt	R. Spielmann	P. S. Leonhardt	R. Spielmann
1 P-K4	P-K4	5 KPxP	QxP
2 N-KB3	N-QB3	6 PxP	B-N5
3 P-Q4	PxP	7 B-K2	N-B3
4 P-B3	P-Q4	8 N-B3	Q-KR4

8 . . . B-N5 used to be played frequently, but the move is bad: there follows 9 O-O, and Black has the disagreeable choice of playing . . . KBxN or moving the Queen after all, thus admitting that 8 . . . B-N5 was useless.

9 O-O   . . . .

A trifle heedless. He should develop the Queen-side: B-K3, R-B1, Q-N3.

9 . . . .   B-Q3   10 P-KR3   . . . .

Both parties have deliberately played for this position on the correct assumption that Black's Queen Bishop cannot move

away now because White obtains the advantage with 11 N-K5. This is also the case after 10 ... BxP?; but the following move —albeit the only one—is good.

| 10 | .... | O-O-O | 11 | PxB? | .... |

Consistent but risky. The sacrifice is of the passive type and can be declined without disadvantage. For this purpose 11 N-QN5 is the most suitable move, as it eliminates one of the dangerous Bishops.

After the move in the text, Black obtains a very violent attack which succeeds without the first player making a demonstrable mistake.

| 11 | .... | NxNP |

Now Black threatens to win with 12 . . . B-R7ch and 13 . . . NxQP.

12 P-KN3! . . . .

The only defense. In the book of the tournament, which praises White's play to this point, it is erroneously asserted that White can win here with 12 R-K1. Even the variation given as proof of this contention is unclear: 12 R-K1, NxQP; 13 QxN, B-R7ch; 14 K-B1, RxQ; 15 NxR, for with Queen and two Pawns against Rook and two minor pieces, Black does not as yet have a lost game.

But the only reply to 12 R-K1 considered by the book of the tournament is 12 . . . NxQP. Actually, Black has a win with 12 . . . B-R7ch! (very important—it is essential to drive the King to B1); 13 K-B1 (13 K-R1? allows mate in four, beginning with 13 . . . B-N6 dis ch), B-K4! and now Black threatens 14 . . . Q-R8ch and 15 . . . N-R7 mate. If now 14 K-N1, Black has a deadly intensification of the attack in 14 . . . NxQP.

But without interpolating the check at R7, 12 . . . B-K4 is as bad as 12 . . . NxQP; for White can simply play 13 PxB.

In making these remarks, I have no intention of indulging in polemics against Dr. Tarrasch, the author of the book of the tournament. Rather does the case appear instructive to me in that it demonstrates that at times even great masters have little faith in the real sacrifice. Dr. Tarrasch was undoubtedly my superior as a master, but he was not partial to bold sacrifices and was therefore prejudiced.

12 . . . . Q-R6!

Here the Queen occupies an exceptionally strong position and cripples White's game. His King Knight is tied down, nor can his King Rook move, as then 13 . . . BxP decides at once. Consequently there is no possibility of driving off the Black pieces from their strong points. Various reinforcements of the attack are threatened: ... P-KR4-5 or 13 ... BxP. Hence White's next move.

| 13 N-K4 | B-K2 |

Threatens 14 ... NxQP.

| 14 B-K3 | P-B4 | 15 QN-Q2 | .... |

There is nothing else, for if 15 QN-N5, BxN; 16 BxB, NxQP and wins. 15 N-B3 loses even more rapidly after 15 ... NxB.

| 15 .... | NxB | 16 PxN | QxPch |
| | | 17 K-R1 | R-Q3 |

Nothing can be devised against this.

| 18 N-R2 | R-R3 | 19 B-R5 | .... |

Desperation. If 19 QN-B3, B-Q3 wins for Black.

| 19 .... | B-Q3 | 20 R-B4 | .... |

After 20 Q-K2, QxNch is one of several winning lines.

| 20 .... | BxR | 21 PxB | Q-R5 |
| | | | Resigns |

Black wins another piece.

This game also features an obvious Kings' Field sacrifice, such as happens or might happen constantly. Here also it would have been a mistake to try to explore each and every consequence at the time of sacrificing. It would have been quite impossible under a time limit and probably would have led Black to avoid the risk involved, perhaps with 10 ... BxN? A bad position and the likely loss of the game would have been the result of such thoroughness.

EXAMPLE 28

Vienna Game
Ostend, 1907

WHITE	BLACK	WHITE	BLACK
R. Spielmann	O. Duras	R. Spielmann	O. Duras
1 P-K4	P-K4	2 N-QB3	N-QB3
		3 P-B4	B-B4

Playable, with the proviso that Black should make up his mind to sacrifice a Pawn next move.

4 PxP	BxN?

After this Black drifts into a bad position. With the developing sacrifice 4 . . . P-Q3! introduced subsequently by Schlechter, an approximately equal position is obtained. White cannot very well accept the offer, as Black gets an excellent development after 5 PxP, QxP; 6 N-B3, B-KN5 followed by 7 . . . O-O-O. White must, on the contrary, humbly play 5 N-B3, returning the extra Pawn.

5 RxB	NxP	6 P-Q4	N-N3

Here 6 . . . Q-R5ch? loses a piece. On the next two moves also, the capture of the King Rook Pawn also leads to decisive disadvantage.

7 B-K3	P-Q3	10 O-O-O	O-O
8 Q-B3	B-K3	11 P-KN4	P-KB3
9 B-Q3	KN-K2	12 Q-N3	R-B2
		13 P-KR4	. . . .

The Pawn-storm sets in. Object: line-opening.

13	N-KB1	14 QR-B1	P-B3
		15 P-N5	P-KB4

After a very onerous opening, Duras—as was his wont—has defended with great dexterity and held up the attack. If White exchanges Pawns or simply allows Black to do so, the position is much simplified and the attack fades away. The following Pawn sacrifice crosses Black's plans.

16   P-N6!   . . . .

Here we have a case in which the King's Field sacrifice amounts to only one Pawn. It brings about the opening of a file, but is not a line-clearance sacrifice, as it occurs *within the reach of the Pawns in the King's Field*. White's attack gains considerably in vitality, as the major pieces on the open file become very effective. On these grounds the text move seems to me the most consistent continuation.

In truth there were other good moves, for example 16 P-R5 (16 . . . P-KN3!; 17 B-KB4, P-Q4!); but the King Knight file remains closed, and most of the White pieces must seek new stations in order to attack effectively and without delay. This would be illogical, for the attack must be conducted economically. Once pieces are well-placed, it is far more economical to increase their efficacy by a small sacrifice in material, than to spend much time on the re-grouping of forces for the purpose. The King's Field sacrifice must be assessed from this general point of view.

16	....	RPxP

The only alternative is 16 ... N/B1xP, when 17 B-KN5 follows with the threat of 18 P-R5. If Black plays 17 . . . PxP; 18 NxP threatens Q6 and gives White a splendid attack. If 17 . . . P-B5 White need not capture at once but retires 18 Q-R2, recapturing the Pawn afterwards in even better circumstances.

17 P-R5! ....

This Pawn obviously cannot be taken because of 17 ... NPxP; 18 PxP, B-Q2 (if 18 . . . NxP?; 19 BxN, BxB; 20 RxB!); 19 P-B6 etc.

17	....	BPxP	19	BxP	P-Q4
18	RxR	BxR	20	B-Q3	Q-Q2

21 B-Q2 ....

An exchange was threatened by 21 . . . N-B4. Observe the excellent disposition of White's troops: the Queen, Rook and Bishop especially have benefited by the sacrifice.

21	....	N-B4	22 Q-N5	N-K2

White was threatening 23 PxP etc. Black had an alternative

in 22 . . . Q-K3, but he wishes to preserve this square for his minor pieces.

23   N-K2   . . . .

Threatening 24 N-B4. The pressure on the Knight file is gradually becoming unbearable.

23   . . . .   N-K3   24   Q-N2   P-KN4

Black no longer has any satisfactory moves. 24 . . . PxP? as well as 24 . . . N-KB1 fails on account of 25 N-B4! On the other hand, something had to be done about the threat of 25 PxP.

25   BxP   BxP

After 25 . . . NxB; 26 QxN Black loses even more rapidly, as the mate threat can only be parried by 26 . . . P-KN3.

26   B-B6!   . . . .

There is no good reply to this. Among other things, White threatens 27 B-K5 and 28 N-B4.

| 26 | . . . . | BxN | 28 | B-K5 | R-B2 |
| 27 | QxB | R-KB1 | 29 | Q-R5 | . . . . |

An ideal position. The threatened mate can only be staved off by heavy sacrifices. If 29 . . . N-KB1; 30 R-R1.

| 29 | . . . . | K-B1 | 31 | B-R7 | K-K1 |
| 30 | Q-R8ch | N-N1 | 32 | BxN | Resigns |

EXAMPLE 29

Ruy Lopez
Match, 1932

WHITE	BLACK	WHITE	BLACK
R. Spielmann	E. Bogolyubov	R. Spielmann	E. Bogolyubov
1 P-K4	P-K4	5 Q-K2	B-K2
2 N-KB3	N-QB3	6 P-B3	P-Q3
3 B-N5	P-QR3	7 P-Q4	B-Q2
4 B-R4	N-B3	8 O-O	O-O
		9 B-B2	....

Black was threatening 9 . . . NxQP!

9   ....   R-K1

Bogolyubov usually plays 9 . . . B-N5 or 9 . . . PxP.

10 P-Q5	N-N1	11 P-KR3	P-B3
		12 PxP	....

The system based on 10 P-Q5 and 12 PxP appeals to me
White obtains fine possibilities for his pieces.

12   ....   BxBP

Of the three possible methods of capture, this is the weakest. Rubinstein, a great judge of this defense, always took with the Knight.

13 P-B4!	QN-Q2	14 N-B3	N-B4
		15 P-QN4	N-K3

If Bogolyubov had this Knight maneuver in mind when playing 12 . . . BxBP, he nevertheless overestimated its efficacy.

16 B-K3	B-B1	17 KR-Q1	Q-B1
		18 QR-B1	P-QN4

The only chance of obtaining some counterplay in this rather constricted position. If White captures twice on QN5, he loses his Queen Rook Pawn.

19 N-Q5!	Q-N2	20 N-R4	. . . .

Stronger than 20 NxNch, for the Knight is strong at Q5 and in any event cannot be exchanged by Black without disadvantage.

20	N-Q2	21 PxP	QxP

If 21 . . . BxP; 22 Q-N4, and if 21 . . . PxP; 22 B-N3. The exchange of Queens is of course welcomed by Black.

22 B-Q3	Q-N2	24 R-K1	P-N3
23 B-QB4	B-R5	25 Q-N4	QR-B1
		26 N-B5	P-KR4

With this last move the second player has weakened his King's Field still further. Yet the move cannot be called a mistake, as no better continuation is in sight. 26 . . . B-N4 would only have meaning if, after 27 B-N3, RxR; 28 RxR Black could play 28 . . . R-B1. But this is not the case because of the reply 29 N-K7ch [or simply 29 RxR].

Hence 26 . . . B-N4 only brings the Bishop on to an unfavorable square, where, after 27 B-N3, it must expect the advance P-QR4, coupled with the eventual surrender of the Queen Bishop file—an altogether negative result.

27 Q-B3!   . . . .

Stronger than 27 Q-N3, as White obtains a most dangerous pressure on the King Bishop file.

It is also stronger than 27 Q-R4 (despite the threat of 28 N-K7ch), which has the same effect as the text if the sacrifice is accepted at once. But Black replies 27 . . . RxB!; 28 RxR, PxN; 29 PxP, QxN; 30 PxN, QxKP maintaining the advantage.

The text move 27 Q-B3 is allied to a passive King's Field sacrifice in that the Knight is left *en prise*. It is a sacrifice of a piece which every experienced player will deem correct at the first glance, but which cannot be calculated accurately over the board under a time limit. In such cases, positional judgment must be the final authority. This point of view is not, as it may seem, entirely subjective; it is based, to a large extent, on practical considerations, such as easing nervous strain and saving time. In fact, I made the move without thinking very long about it, and it is significant that my opponent did not take much time to decline the offer.

If lengthy subsequent investigation has established that the

sacrifice was beyond cavil and could not have been accepted
by the second player without aggravating his difficulties—
so much the better! This does not constitute a reason for
classifying the combination as a sham sacrifice. Let us define
the difference yet again: sham sacrifices are those the success of which can be clearly foreseen, or—to allow for human
imperfection!—could be foreseen, from the critical move on-
wards. Real sacrifices are those which cannot be gauged
exactly in practical play, and can only be estimated. It is true
that no hard and fast line of demarcation can be drawn between the two, as it would vary according to the skill of the
player. But the objective standpoint is not of paramount importance for our purpose, as, after all, every player has to
depend on his own capabilities.

In advocating at all times in this book my own line of
thought and my own convictions, I make allowance for relative conceptions about sacrifices, and hope to stimulate the
student to play subjectively.

After this digression, we return to the game:

27   ....   R-B3

The acceptance of the sacrifice would probably mean insuperable difficulties for Black, thus: 27 . . . PxN; 28 PxP
(threatening to win back the piece, in addition to threatening
to win the Queen), N-Q1?; 29 QxP and Black has no adequate
defense against the numerous threats—above all 30 P-B6. If,
for example, 29 . . . B-N2; 30 B-R6 (threatening 31 Q-N5)
wins as well as 30 P-B6.

But after 27 . . . PxN; 28 PxP, Black has a better defense than 28 . . . N-Q1?—namely 28 . . . B-B3. Then, after
29 PxN, PxP; 30 N-B6ch, NxN; 31 QxN, P-Q4; 32 B-K2,
White's prospects are favorable, but not entirely clear-cut and
hence not so assured as after the text.

If White had played 27 Q-N3, Black could have replied 27

. . . K-R2 with an appreciable lessening of his troubles. However, in the text continuation (after 27 Q-B3!), 27 . . . K-R2 is immediately refuted by 28 NxP, BxN; 29 QxBPch followed by 30 N-B6(ch) etc.

28   N-R6ch   . . . .

This check, made possible by the offer of the Knight, secures White the advantage of the two Bishops.

28   . . . .   BxN   29   BxB   . . . .

29   . . . .   N-Q5?

After this mistake, Black's game collapses at once. But there was no longer a sufficient defense.

29 . . . Q-B1 has been said to be the best move here. It may be so against either 30 N-K3, B-N4!—or 30 B-Q3, N-Q5 (31 N-B6ch, K-R1!) which is not desirable from White's point of view. 30 Q-Q3 is more favorable, as White maintains his positional advantage (two Bishops and the Queen-side majority).

But by far the strongest reply to 29 . . . Q-B1 is 30 Q-R3! setting Black a problem which he cannot solve. The reason lies in the fact that after 30 . . . RxB; 31 QxB, the threats 32 QxN!, or 32 RxR followed by 33 QxN, arise, against which there is no satisfactory defense. If the threatened Knight

moves, a Rook is lost. 31 . . . N/K3-B1 likewise fails, for after
32 RxR, QxR; 33 BxN a piece is lost. [*Nor can Black play
31 . . . RxR; 32 RxR, Q-Q1; 33 QxN!*]

It follows that Black, after 30 Q-R3!, cannot capture the
Bishop. He must play 30 . . . B-N4, after which follows
31 BxB, PxB; 32 Q-R7! with the renewed threat of QxN etc.
This can only be parried by 32 . . . N/K3-B1 and there follows 33 RxR, QxR; 34 R-QB1, Q-R1; 35 Q-B7—or 35 R-B7—
with a hopeless position for Black.

Possibly Black might interpolate 30 . . . K-R2 (after
30 Q-R3!); but very much the same variation arises after
31 B-K3, B-N4; while 31 . . . RxB; 32 QxB, N/K3-B1 is answered victoriously by 33 Q-N3!, RxR; 34 N-B6ch!, NxN;
35 QxPch, K-R1; 36 QxN/B6ch and 37 RxR.

| 30 | N-B6ch! | . . . . |

It is easy to see that this Knight cannot be taken.

| 30 | . . . . | K-R1 | 31 | B-N7ch | . . . . |

Bogolyubov had overlooked this pleasantry in his calculations. The play is over.

| 31 | . . . . | KxB | 32 | NxRch | K-R3 |
| | | | 33 | QxBP | Resigns |

EXAMPLE 30

Queen's Gambit Declined
Vienna, 1926

WHITE	BLACK	WHITE	BLACK
A. Becker	R. Spielmann	A. Becker	R. Spielmann
1 P-Q4	P-Q4	3 P-B4	P-B3
2 N-KB3	N-KB3	4 P-K3	B-B4
		5 QN-Q2	. . . .

White should try to fight against 4 . . . B-B4; for which purpose 5 PxP is appropriate.

5	P-K3	6 B-K2	B-Q3
		7 P-B5	....

More elastic is the development of the Queen Bishop by 7 P-QN3 and 8 B-N2.

7	B-B2	8 P-QN4	QN-Q2
		9 B-N2	Q-K2

Preparing for . . . P-K4: the adversary's wing attack is to be countered as rapidly as possible by an undertaking in the center. 9 . . . N-K5 was the alternative.

10 O-O	P-K4	11 PxP	....

Else 11 . . . P-K5 follows, with preponderant King-side prospects for Black.

11	NxKP	12 N-Q4	....

White refuses to simplify. The Knight is excellently placed here; but Black's minor pieces, aiming at White's King, are a lasting menace.

12	B-Q2

At KN3 this Bishop is exposed to the advance of White's King Bishop Pawn.

13 Q-B2	N/K4-N5	14 P-KR3	N-R3

This move guards Black's KB4, leaves the road to K4 free for Black's Queen and already toys with various sacrificial possibilities, such as 15 P-N4?, N/B3xP! etc.

15 B-Q3	O-O	16 KR-K1	....

Weakens the King's Field. 16 QR-K1 is more prudent.

16 ....   KR-K1   17 Q-B3   ....

In order to refute 17 . . . N-K5? by 18 BxN, PxB; 19 NxBP.

17 ....   Q-K4   18 P-B4   ....

Bold, but undoubtedly stronger than passive defense by
18 N/Q4-B3 or 18 N-B1, after which the same move follows
as in the game.

18 ....   Q-R4

White has laid out his game in very incisive fashion, and
his attacking prospects are not to be underestimated. If he
succeeds, after suitable preparation, in unleashing his King
Knight Pawn as well, he will most likely obtain a decisive
advantage. For the moment, however, his King-side is only
weakened by the Pawn moves to KB4 and KR3. It is a question of Black's turning these weak points to account before
they are made strong. A favorable opportunity will offer after
White's next move.

19 N/Q4-B3?   ....

Instead of this, White can try to trap Black's Queen, but
without success: 19 B-K2, Q-R5; 20 N/Q4-B3, Q-N6; 21 N-B1,
Q-N3; 22 B-Q3, N-K5!—or 22 N-R4, Q-K5 etc.

The right play is 19 N-B1!, after which the following sacrifice is inadequate.

| 19 | .... | BxRP! | 20 PxB | QxP |

Again an everyday King's Field sacrifice: KR3 on either side is a favorite sacrificial point. The stake is small, as the piece given up is almost offset by the gain of two Pawns. What matters, in such cases, is whether or not the attack or at least the pressure against the hostile position can be kept up after the sacrifice. It will be quite essential to support the Queen at KR6 so that she can stay within striking distance of the King's Field.

Nothing is more ominous for an attacker than the compulsory retreat of his most powerful unit; for then the counter-attack, undertaken with an extra piece, usually becomes irresistible.

In the present case, all the general premises of a sound sacrifice are manifested in profusion. Black's strongly posted Queen can be quickly assisted by at least a Knight. In addition there is powerful pressure on the King file, where White's King Pawn offers a welcome object of attack.

21   R-K2?   ....

This mistake enables Black to strengthen his attack decisively. It is essential to bring back the King Bishop for the defense. After 21 B-KB1!, Q-N6ch; 22 B-N2, N/R3-N5; 23 N-B1, Q-B7ch, Black maintains a strong attack—without, however, having immediately decisive continuations at his disposal. On 23 R-K2, BxP? fails because of 24 N-B1; but 23 . . . RxP!; 24 N-B1, RxQ; 25 NxQ, R-B5 is permissible and good for Black.

[*See diagram on page 142.*]

21   ....   BxP!?

A tempting combination, which is not bad and which actually leads to a beautiful final attack. But it cannot be viewed as the best continuation, White being in a position to decline the additional sacrifice with the gain of a tempo.

The most compelling continuation, though difficult to calculate in all its ramifications, is the simple and obvious move 21 . . . N/R3-N5; after this, any attempt to keep the all-important King Pawn protected by 22 QR-K1 or 22 Q-Q4 fails because of 22 . . . RxP!, when White's Rook on K2 cannot leave the second rank because of the ensuing mate in two. On the other hand, abandoning the threatened King Pawn without a struggle is tantamount to a total collapse of White's game, for Black—apart from the point of view of material—obtains a decisive advantage through his control of all the lines of attack.

The attempt at indirect protection (after 21 . . . N/R3-N5!) by 22 B-B5 is also unsatisfactory; there follows 22 . . . BxP; 23 BxN, QxBch; 24 R-N2, BxPch; 25 K-B1, Q-R6 (26 QxN, QxRch!) etc.

As the King Pawn cannot be supported after 21 . . . N/R3-N5!, White must seek salvation in counterattack. Such an opportunity lies in the maneuver 22 R-N2, RxP; 23 N-N5,

Q-R3 (releasing the Knight by guarding KN2. Other Queen moves are even worse); 24 NxRP! and White obtains an irresistible attack.

This counterplay is very fine—but not forced. Instead of immediately capturing the King Pawn, Black must interpolate a line-clearance sacrifice: 21 . . . N/R3-N5!; 22 R-N2, P-Q5!!; 23 QxP (clearly compulsory; hopeless would be 23 PxP, or 23 NxP, or 23 Q-B4, QxRch!), QR-Q1; 24 Q-B3 (again forced), and only now 24 . . . RxP!; 25 N-N5, Q-R4! (without the line-clearance sacrifice, this move is insufficient because of BxPch and Q-Q4. But now it wins); 26 NxRP, R-R6!; 27 NxNch, PxN and White cannot save the game.

> 22 PxB?   . . . .

After this the combination works. White should decline the second sacrifice with 22 Q-Q4! This gains a valuable tempo, and at the least, makes possible a more protracted resistance than after 21 . . . N/R3-N5! (discussed in the previous note).

> 22 . . . .   RxR   23 BxR   Q-N6ch
> 24 K-R1   . . . .

After 24 K-B1 the main feature of the second Bishop sacrifice comes to light: 24 . . . N/R3-N5; 25 Q-Q4, R-K1 and there is no defense against the coming Knight check at K6.

> 24 . . . .   N/R3-N5   25 R-KB1   . . . .

The only reasonable way to parry the threatened mate. This is as far as I calculated the second sacrifice, observing that at worst I have a perpetual check.

> 25 . . . .   Q-R6ch   26 K-N1   Q-N6ch

In order to gain time on the clock. After all, Black is two pieces down and the slightest miscalculation may be fatal. He is not renouncing the perpetual check until he finds a clear win.

27   K-R1   R-K1!

Forcing White's next move: if the attacked Bishop moves, then the pretty reply 28 . . . R-K8! decides the issue. The Rook cannot then be captured because of mate on the move, so that the impending 29 . . . N-B7 mate leads to the win of White's Queen.

28   Q-Q3   Q-R6ch

Another repetition of moves to gain time for examining the winning process. The point is to find the quickest of several available winning methods.

29   K-N1   Q-N6ch   30   K-R1   . . . .

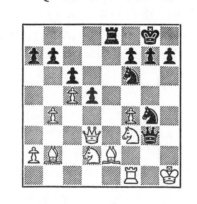

30   . . . .   Q-R6ch?

Careless play, after which the shortest winning method is no longer feasible. This was 30 . . . N-R4! with the two main threats 31 . . . Q-R6ch followed by 32 . . . N-N6; or 31 . . . NxP. Black overlooks that after the text move he cannot again play . . . Q-N6ch, as a draw by repetition of moves arises automatically.

31 K-N1   N-K6

If 31 . . . N-R4, White has the resource 32 QxPch, KxQ; 33 N-N5ch, which, however, does not save the game: 33 . . . K-N1; 34 NxQ, RxB; 35 B-B1 (the only move; 35 B-B3?, P-Q5! or 35 R-Q1?, N-K6! loses more rapidly for White), N-K6!; 36 R-B3 (if 36 R-B2?, R-K8ch), R-N7ch; 37 K-R1, N-N6ch and Black, with Rook and two Pawns against two minor pieces, maintains the attack with the well-founded prospect of winning further Pawns.

However, the continuation chosen leads to a quicker decision.

32 N-K1   . . . .

Forced. If 32 R-B2, Q-N6ch; 33 K-R1, QxR; 34 B-KB1, N-R4! etc. And if 32 K-B2, mate in three follows by 32 . . . N/B3-N5ch; 33 K-K1, Q-N6ch etc.

32 . . . .   Q-N6ch   33 K-R1   Q-R6ch

Again playing for time to seek the best winning method.

34 K-N1   Q-N6ch   35 K-R1   NxR
                             36 BxN   . . . .

Or 36 NxN, QxN.

36 . . . .   R-K6   37 Q-B5   RxN
                             38 B-K5   . . . .

Or 38 BxN, PxB; 39 QxBP, R-Q8!; 40 Q-Q4, Q-K8! and Black wins a piece, for if 41 Q-B6, simply 41 . . . RxN; 42 Q-Q8ch, K-N2; 43 Q-N5ch, K-B1 followed in due course by . . . Q-K1.

38 . . . .   Q-N5

At last the exchange of Queens is favorable. White must comply, as 39 . . . N-R4 is threatened.

39   QxQ   NxQ

Black now wins a piece, as nothing can be done against the threat of 40 . . . R-Q8; 41 B-B3, P-Q5.

40   K-N2   R-Q8
Resigns

Many more examples of the King's Field sacrifice could be given, but we must confine ourselves to those given here. Bearing in mind the many different forms this sacrifice can assume, we must refrain from enumerating all the circumstances which can lead to it. The most frequent causes are all kinds of weaknesses in the hostile position and inadequate protection of the King's Field by pieces.

KING-HUNT SACRIFICES

The object of this sacrifice is to chase the King out into the open on a full board. The problem composers speak of the sacrifice which draws the King into a mating net. If it did not sound so incongruous, the King-Hunt sacrifice might be termed the "driving-out" sacrifice.

The King's weal or woe is the "be-all and end-all" of everything that happens on the chessboard. Therefore one achieves a distinct success by forcing the enemy King out into the open. To bring this about, it is permissible to offer big sacrifices of material. This principle is familiar to us from former chapters.

The attempt to bring the King into a dangerous situation can be made in two ways: either the forces protecting him are eliminated or decimated, or the King is compelled to leave his stronghold and to wander forth alone into the wilderness.

We have encountered the first of these methods on several previous occasions, especially in connection with sacrifices in the King's Field. This chapter is devoted to the second process.

It needs little reflection to realize that the King, when driven out into the open, is exposed to far more serious dangers than when assailed in his own fortress. This becomes particularly evident when we count up tempi. In three moves the King can reach the middle rank, where, on a full board, he is as a rule helpless. Such a defenseless state can never come about in so few moves when the King is attacked in his own "hideout."

This stands to reason. In one case, the King comes out to meet his assailants, thus saving them much trouble; in the other, the attacking forces must march a long way and engage in a rough-and-tumble with the defenders before they can reach the King. It follows that each tempo spent by the King in his flight into the open, will mean several tempi saved by the attackers!

Furthermore, it can readily be seen that the detrimental effect of the tempi spent by the King rises progressively, the farther the King strays into the open and the longer he stays there. If, for example, he has to enter the second rank during the middle game, there is, in most cases, little to be feared. But let him enter the third rank and he is in great danger. For him to advance to the fourth rank—let alone further—is, nearly without exception, fatal.

Even when the King, after reaching the open, weathers the immediate storm, the danger is by no means over. For he cannot maintain himself indefinitely outside the wall of his own Pawn structure and he must therefore wander to find a safe haven; the demands of development and other positional requirements must for a time be neglected. And so it can happen that, although the King may reach the sanctuary he was making for, the catastrophe still comes to pass: either the refuge is no longer snug enough to resist the oncoming foe, or the position collapses because of weaknesses elsewhere.

We see from the foregoing that the King-Hunt promises results greater than any of the other real sacrifices treated up to now. Consequently it can, in principle, afford proportionately greater stakes.

EXAMPLE 31

Dutch Defense
San Sebastian, 1912

WHITE	BLACK	WHITE	BLACK
A. Rubinstein	R. Spielmann	A. Rubinstein	R. Spielmann
1 P-Q4	P-K3	4 B-Q2	N-KB3
2 P-QB4	P-KB4	5 P-KN3	O-O
3 N-QB3	B-N5	6 B-N2	P-Q3
		7 P-QR3	. . . .

Loss of time. Black has to exchange at his QB6 sooner or later. Better 7 N-B3.

7	BxN	9 Q-B2	P-B4
8 BxB	QN-Q2	10 PxP	. . . .

Weak. Black's Queen Knight now gets effectively into the game. There were several better moves, for example 10 N-B3 or R-Q1 or—perhaps best of all—10 P-K3.

10	NxP	12 O-O	B-Q2
11 N-B3	N/B4-K5	13 KR-Q1	. . . .

Better 13 QR-Q1.

13	R-B1

[See diagram on page 149.]

14 BxN   . . .

Necessary. Had White played 13 QR-Q1, he could now support his Queen Bishop Pawn by 14 N-Q2.

But with the Rooks placed as they are in the diagram position, 14 N-Q2? (instead of 14 BxN) gives rise to a decisive combination: 14 . . . NxBP!; 15 KxN, N-N5ch; 16 K-B3, B-B3ch; 17 P-K4, Q-N4—or 16 K-K1, Q-N3!, winning in either case. If White interpolates 15 BxN before accepting the sacrifice, then 15 . . . Q-N3! proves decisive.

| 14 | .... | QxB | 15 | Q-N3 | QR-B2 |
| | | | 16 | N-K1 | .... |

16 N-Q2 provides a better defense, the object being to reply to 16 . . . N-B4 with 17 Q-B2 without losing the exchange by 17 . . . B-R5.

If 16 QR-B1, Black plays 16 . . . KR-B1 with the strong threat . . . P-QN4.

| 16 | .... | N-B4 | 17 | Q-N4 | P-B5! |

Black has the superior position. After the opening of the King Bishop file, he will soon be threatening a direct attack.

| 18 | N-Q3 | .... |

Likewise after 18 N-B3, PxP; 19 RPxP, P-K4 Black secures a violent attack.

| 18 | .... | PxP | 19 | BPxP | NxN |
| | | | 20 | RxN | .... |

20 PxN, Q-Q5ch; 21 K-R1, B-B3; 22 BxB, PxB; 23 R-KB1 (or 23 Q-B3, Q-K6), QR-B2 is also clearly in Black's favor.

20 ....   Q-B7ch   21 K-R1   B-B3!

Much better than 21 . . . QxKP with the probable continuation 22 R-Q2, QxP; 23 QxQ, RxQ; 24 RxP, B-B3; 25 BxB followed by 26 R-Q2 with considerable drawing chances.

Besides threatening mate at KB8, the move in the text also contains the trap 22 BxB?, QxKP! and wins.

22 P-K4   QR-B2!

After this, White cannot capture the Queen Pawn—not with the Queen because of 23 . . . Q-K7!, nor with the Rook because of 23 . . . BxP!; 24 BxB, Q-K7! etc.

23 R-KB1? is also immediately fatal because of 23 . . . QxRch!

23 R-K1   P-QR4!

Black's Queen wishes to get out of the path of her own Rooks and seeks a suitable square for the purpose. Therefore the hostile Queen is to be diverted first from protecting her Queen Bishop Pawn.

24 Q-B3   ....

If 24 QxRP, there follows—as mentioned before—not 24 . . . QxQNP, when Black can obtain some relief by 25 R-Q2, driving back the Black Queen, or forcing the exchange of Queens after 25 . . . Q-N6; 26 Q-N4.

Best after 24 QxRP is 24 . . . Q-B7! If then White plays 25 R-Q2, QxBP can follow, threatening 26 . . . R-B8ch etc. The seemingly better move 25 Q-B3? is refuted prettily by 25 . . . BxP! threatening among other things, mate by 26 . . . R-B8ch etc.

24 ....   Q-QB4   25 P-QN4   ....

Rubinstein, who has conducted the defense in difficult circumstances as well as possible, tries with his last move to enforce complete freedom and even give the game a turn in his favor. If Black's Queen now had to give way, the Queen Pawn would be lost or the endgame resulting from 25 . . . Q-K4 would be in White's favor.

However, Black enters upon a combination which has been dormant for some time and has played a part in several variations. It cannot be calculated down to the last detail, and can only be gauged intuitively; but I had full confidence. It only remains to point out that White's last move is more or less compulsory, for with any other continuation Black can at the least increase his advantage by quiet position play, such as, for example, . . . P-R5.

25 . . . . BxP!

The crowning point of this complicated sacrifice lies in the fact that through the sacrifice of a whole Rook the hostile King is forced into the open. It is therefore a King-Hunt sacrifice. I could not calculate the combination more exactly, and I had to rely entirely on my conviction that favorable variations would occur as a matter of course. And events proved me to be right.

26 RxB . . . .

Of course White cannot take the Queen, as mate is threatened at his KB1.

But instead of the move in the text, 26 BxB suggests itself. The continuation would be: 26 . . . R-B8ch; 27 RxR, RxRch; 28 K-N2, R-N8ch; 29 K-B3, Q-R4ch; 30 K-K3, QxP; and White, although a piece up, is in great and probably insurmountable difficulties on account of the exposed position of his King. It would be a problem in itself to examine the position more closely. But from the practical standpoint, which in our sense, should alone hold the scales in judging real sacrifices, only an estimate is possible. In my opinion, it should prove favorable to the second player. He who would not boldly undertake to win such a position with Black, will never go far in the domain of the sacrifice!

Comparatively the best defense—as indicated by subsequent analysis—is 26 R-B3, with the continuation 26 . . . PxP; 27 PxP, Q-B3; 28 P-N5 (if 28 RxB?, QxR; 29 RxR, Q-N8ch), RxR!; 29 QxR!, BxQ; 30 PxQ, BxBch; 31 KxB, PxP; 32 RxP, R-B3; 33 R-K7, when White, with a Pawn down, has some slight drawing chances.

In the continuation which actually occurs, we get the main variation of the sacrifice.

26	....	R-B8ch	28	K-N2	Q-B7ch
27	BxR	RxBch	29	K-R3	R-KR8!

This is as far as the combination was calculated. Black is a Rook down, but he drives the King up to the fourth rank. Such an attack must succeed! But 29 . . . Q-B4ch is useless because of 30 K-N2.

After the move in the text, 30 . . . Q-B4ch is a real threat, 31 K-N2? being impossible because of 31 . . . Q-B8 mate.

30   R-B3   ....

Relatively best, though it is as inadequate as other defenses.

| 30 | .... | QxRPch | 32 | K-B4 | Q-R3ch |
| 31 | K-N4 | Q-R4ch | 33 | K-N4 | P-KN4! |

Threatening 34 . . . Q-R4 mate and thus forcing White to give back the Rook.

34 RxP ....

The only other plausible move 34 R-B8ch is palpably weaker. However, the text move is only an ephemeral resource; Black's attack remains substantially the same. This is frequently observed in sacrificial attacks. From this we conclude: *the repulse of a sacrificial attack which has been initiated in a superior position, will cost the defender greater sacrifices, generally speaking, than the attacker has made; merely returning the material given up, will rarely suffice.*

| 34 | .... | QxRch | 35 | R-B5 | .... |

35 KxP also loses: 35 . . . P-R3ch; 36 K-B4, R-K8!

I. 37 R-K3, R-B8ch; 38 R-B3, Q-B2ch; 39 K-K4 (or 39 K-N4, RxR; 40 QxR, QxPch etc.), RxR; 40 QxR, QxPch with a forced exchange of Queens and a won Pawn ending for Black.

II. 37 Q-Q4, Q-B2ch; 38 K-N4, Q-N3ch; 39 K-R3, Q-R4ch; 40 K-N2, Q-R8ch; 41 K-B2, Q-N8 mate.

35   ....   P-R3

With the idea of winning by . . . K-R2-N3. A little more precise was the following line: 35 . . . Q-K5ch; 36 KxP, P-R3ch; 37 K-B6 (if 37 K-N6, Q-K1ch etc), R-K8!; 38 K-N6, Q-N5ch etc.

| 36 | Q-Q3 | K-N2 | 37 | K-B3 | .... |

Or 37 Q-Q5, P-R4ch; 38 K-B3, R-B8ch winning.

37   ....   R-B8ch!

Forcing a general exchange.

38   QxR   ....

Or 38 K-N4, P-R4ch!; 39 KxNP, Q-N3ch and mate next move.

38	....	QxRch	41	PxP	K-B3
39	K-N2	QxQch	42	K-B2	P-R4
40	KxQ	PxP		Resigns	

EXAMPLE 32

Queen's Gambit Declined
Vienna, 1933

WHITE	BLACK	WHITE	BLACK
R. Spielmann	S. Rubinstein	R. Spielmann	S. Rubinstein

1	P-Q4	N-KB3	4	N-B3	B-K2
2	P-QB4	P-K3	5	B-N5	O-O
3	N-QB3	P-Q4	6	P-K3	P-QN3

An antiquated defense. Better is . . . QN-Q2.

| 7 | B-Q3 | B-N2 | 9 | PxP | PxP |
| 8 | BxN | BxB | 10 | P-KR4! | |

As in the game Marshall-Burn, Paris, 1900, which White won in brilliant style.

10 .... P-B4?

In the game mentioned above, Burn played here 10 . . . P-N3? and succumbed to a deadly attack. The text move, being too challenging, is likewise not good. 10 P-KR4! clearly indicated that White has an eye on the sacrifice at KR7. Black must be psychologically in the same predicament as Dekker in Example 26. Accustomed to the fact that the Bishop sacrifice at KR7 is nearly always a sham sacrifice leading to an immediate decision, Black looks for such a variation and, not finding it, concludes that the sacrifice is necessarily unsound.

Reasoning along these lines, we might conclude that the advance of the Queen Bishop Pawn is logical and at all events superior to Burn's timid 10 . . . P-N3?, which weakened the King-side catastrophically. From the analytical point of view—justifiable, for instance, in a postal game—10 . . . P-B4? may even be good. But Black gives too little consideration to the practical dangers to which he exposes himself by conjuring up the sacrifice. His King will be driven out to at least the third rank, a most alarming state of affairs. It is my opinion—perhaps in opposition to other authors—that one should expose oneself to such perils only under stress of extreme necessity.

I cannot emphasize often enough that, *in practical play, the scale is turned not by the objective state of affairs, but rather by the relative difficulty of the problem which has to be solved.* If the task is particularly arduous, then the player will generally fail, even if, objectively, matters are in his favor.

This applies especially to the defense, which on technical and strategical grounds, as well as for psychological reasons, is far more difficult to conduct than the attack. Hence my conviction that a sacrifice must be appraised not only from the point of view of its soundness, but chiefly from that of the dangers connected with it. For the attacker, it will be profitable to risk such sacrifices; as for the defender, he does well to avoid them as far as possible.

For all these reasons, 10 . . . R-K1 is more advisable. The move is not wholly satisfactory, because 11 Q-B2 forces a loosening of the King-side by 11 . . . P-KR3, after which White can start a violent attack with 12 O-O-O followed by P-KN4. However, in that case, Black's defense is much easier than in the actual game.

> 11 BxPch!   KxB   12 N-N5ch   K-R3

Forced. After (a) 12 . . . BxN?; 13 PxB dis ch or (b) 12 . . . K-N1?; 13 Q-R5 or (c) 12 . . . K-N3?; 13 Q-Q3ch, White wins out of hand.

> 13 Q-Q3   P-N3

Seemingly White's attack has been beaten back: one gathers the impression that the Bishop sacrifice is unsound. Black needs one or two moves to consolidate his position fully and simply hold on to the extra piece.

But the momentarily bad position of Black's King gives the aggressor an opportunity for a second sacrifice.

[*See diagram on page 157.*]

14 P-R5! . . . .

The only way, but a very effective one, to restrain Black's King from attaining security. Not only 15 PxP dis ch is threatened, but above all 15 NxPch!

The one plausible method of declining the sacrifice is 14 . . . K-N2; 15 RPxP, R-R1. But then comes 16 NxBP!, RxRch; 17 K-Q2, RxR; 18 NxQ, BxN (or 18 . . . B-B1; 19 NxP, BxN; 20 Q-K4); 19 Q-B5, B-KB3; 20 Q-R5 and White must win.

14 . . . . BxN

After 14 . . . KxN; 15 P-B4ch!, (a) 15 . . . K-N5; 16 N-Q1, B-R5ch; 17 N-B2ch, BxNch; 18 KxB threatening 19 P-KN3 and 20 R-R4ch or (b) 15 . . . K-R3; 16 PxP dis ch, K-N2; 17 R-R7ch, K-N1; 18 O-O-O followed by 19 QR-R1, the attack succeeds without much difficulty.

15 PxP dis ch K-N2 16 R-R7ch K-B3

The point: Black's King must come out into the open. If 16 . . . K-N1?; 17 PxPch and mate in two more moves.

17 O-O-O! . . . .

With 17 P-B4, White can already win back a piece. But after 17 . . . B-R5ch; 18 RxB, R-R1! Black occupies the King

Rook file, and it is doubtful whether the attack, weakened considerably by the elimination of the advanced Rook, can compensate for even one piece.

After the text move the idea of the combination stands out clearly: these were King-Hunt sacrifices which jointly served no other purpose but to drive the King into the open. The King is so unfavorably placed that he will need several moves in order to reach comparative safety. As the position is open and White has an excellent development, the Black King's journey is fraught with great danger and can hardly be accomplished without serious loss of material.

White can look ahead with confidence. At the moment he has two Pawns, which, from the material point of view, hardly count. But the Pawn at KN6 is very menacing and is destined to play an important part in the attack. That this later happens in the game is not an exceptional case. A Pawn which participates directly in an attack is generally of more value than a whole row of inactive Pawns, which, for the time being, only count from the material point of view. The same conditions concerning the attacking value of Pawns prevail as in the case of pieces.

17　.... 　P-B5

Black intends to bring over his King to the Queen-side and seeks at least to blockade the position there. There is no fault to find with this idea, especially as it can be carried out with the gain of a tempo. As we shall see at once, the text move has other disadvantages. But this is an entirely normal concomitant. In shattered positions, this is always the case: one hole is filled up and another is torn open!

18　Q-K2 　K-K2

Now 19 P-B4, winning back a piece, was already an actual threat.

| 19 | P-B4 | B-B3 | 20 | P-K4! | . . . . |

In consequence of 17 . . . P-B5, this breakthrough in the center is very powerful. Were the Queen Bishop Pawn still at his QB4, White's attack would have to continue in some other way, such as perhaps P-KN4, because the King Pawn would be needed at K3 to guard the square Q4.

| 20 | . . . . | PxP |

Black can in no way allow the White King Pawn to advance further, as the assault by Pawns becomes irresistible: 20 . . . K-K1; 21 P-K5, B-K2; 22 PxPch, K-Q2 (if 22 . . . RxP?; 23 Q-R5); 23 P-KN4 and the four united passed Pawns are, in this exceptional case, stronger than two pieces.

| 21 | NxP | . . . . |

The fact that this Knight cannot be exchanged because of the resulting loss of Black's Queen Rook is very useful for White.

| 21 | . . . . | K-Q2 |

In the course of 21 moves the King has moved seven times (including castling), and still stands badly. This circumstance, typical of the King-Hunt sacrifice, is here clearly manifest.

22　P-Q5　　　N-R3

Black cannot delay his Queen-side development any longer.

23　P-N7!　　. . . .

This Pawn, a standing danger for Black, now advances with decisive effect.

23　. . . .　　　KR-N1

Black cannot stave off grave material loss. If 23 . . . R-K1; 24 P-N8(Q), RxQ; 25 RxPch, B-K2; 26 P-Q6 is crushing.

24　R-R6!　　. . . .

At last the Bishop is overtaken by his long-threatened fate. There is no way out. If 24 . . . B-K2; 25 P-Q6 followed by 26 Q-N4ch, or in the reverse order. To lose this comparatively well-posted piece in such unfavorable circumstances, would have catastrophic consequences. Black therefore decides on a drastic step: he resigns himself to losing his Queen.

24　. . . .　　　BxNP　　　25　R-Q6ch　　　K-B2
　　　　　　　　　　　　　　　26　QxPch!　　. . . .

This is much stronger than the immediate capture of the Queen; for after 26 . . . QRxR, Black brings his King into safety at last and then, with Rook and two Bishops against Queen and two Pawns, he has quite a playable game.

The text move keeps Black's Rooks disconnected.

26　. . . .　　　K-N1

On 26 . . . N-B4 White can even play 27 NxN, QxR (best); 28 N-K4 dis ch, K-Q2; 29 Q-N5ch followed by 30 NxQ.

But the simple continuation 27 RxQ is far more forcing; for if a Rook recaptures, 28 P-QN4 wins a piece, and if 27 . . . KxR; 28 N-Q6 follows. With the powerful Knight still available, White's attack wins with ease.

| 27 | RxQch | RxR | 29 | P-Q6 | N-K3 |
| 28 | K-N1 | N-B2 | 30 | P-B5 | BxNch |

30 . . . R-QB1 is a bit better, but defeat is unavoidable.

31	QxB	N-B4	34	QxP	R-Q2
32	Q-B6	R-QB1	35	Q-N8ch	K-N2
33	Q-Q5	R-Q1	36	Q-Q5ch	K-N1
			37	Q-B6	P-R4

The only defense against the threat 38 P-QN4 etc.

| 38 | QxPch | N-N2 | 39 | Q-B6 | R-Q1 |
| | | | 40 | Q-B7ch | Resigns |

These two games, especially the last, have shown clearly enough to what danger the King is exposed when hunted in the open, and so have proved the advantages of a hunting sacrifice.

In the days of Anderssen—perhaps the greatest sacrificial artist of all time—a King-Hunt sacrifice was no rarity. Numerous games of that period feature a King being chased all over the board and finally getting mated somewhere or other. Frequently such sacrifices turned up right in the opening.

Nowadays, thanks to highly developed technique, King-Hunt sacrifices are rather infrequent. It must be added, however, that this is not to be explained *only* by the fact that the modern player is much more careful in attending to the safety of his King; rather have the principles of modern chess strategy—often no doubt misunderstood!—bred a certain pusillanimity in the conduct of an attack.

I am not deluding myself that this course of evolution can be stemmed by the exposition of a few of my combinative games. But perhaps I shall yet succeed in inspiring some ardent chess disciples with a love for the art of sacrificial play.

2. Sacrificial Values

COMPARED WITH THE *object* OF A SACRIFICE, ITS *size* IS OF SECondary importance.

In order to get at the kernel of the problem, a system had to be evolved for the classification of sacrifices, by which to gauge them from the strategical and tactical point of view. This was done in Part 1.

In Part 2 we shall deal with sacrifices from the point of view of the *values* involved.

The degree of elaboration which was essential when discussing *types*, will not be needed here. For the size of a sacrifice is only an external; the main point will always be its object. At the same time, size and object, as we have pointed out previously, must always be harmoniously interrelated.

First, we have seen that *sham* sacrifices are practically unlimited as to size, for they lead to a forced and profitable recovery of the material given up, or even to a mate. Not so the *real* sacrifice, to which we shall be referring here when saying sacrifice for short.

Where it is a question of overthrowing the adversary by assault (developing, line-clearance or King-Hunt sacrifices), it is at times permissible to risk a great deal of material. But should the object be merely to hinder the opponent's development or to provide a piece with a more favorable square (obstructive, vacating sacrifices), then only in exceptional cases can more than a Pawn be staked.

The most important test by which to assess real sacrifices correctly is an exact knowledge of the varying value of each unit.

This relative value is most noticeable in the case of Pawns. At the beginning of the game, the center Pawns are stronger than those on the wings. Connecting the two sets are the Bishop Pawns, whose value lies between these two extremes. In a scale of relative values, the Rook and Knight Pawns could be represented by 3, the Bishop Pawns by 4 and the King and Queen Pawns by 5.

In the original position, where objects and direction of attack have not yet materialized, the pieces should be developed and made available in any part of the board in the shortest possible time.

This is only possible with a centralized development. The center Pawns are the foundation of such a development. They advance, open up and smooth down the path for the pieces, safeguard their position and secure them against attacks by the hostile Pawns.

All openings, including the modern ones, are based on this principle. Modern theory goes only one step further: the advance of the center Pawns is prepared for by the advance of the Bishop Pawns (P-KB4, P-QB4). It follows that the inside Pawns are of greater value at the beginning of a game than those on the outside. The center Pawns are the shock-troops which open the battle; the others stay behind in reserve and often remain inactive throughout the game.

If intrinsically the Pawns are of unequal value from the very first, their value shifts and changes to a still greater extent in the course of play.

Connected Pawns are inherently more valuable than isolated ones, which does not preclude an isolated Pawn from being very powerful in certain circumstances. Passed Pawns are stronger than others, and passed Pawns supported by their fellows are stronger than those which lack this protection. Advanced passed Pawns are stronger than those which have lagged behind. Two or more united and advanced passed

Pawns are usually an irresistible force, while a Pawn which has reached the last rank can in certain cases be stronger than a Queen.

Take for instance the following position:

White to play

If White makes a Queen, the game is drawn. Let him make a Knight and he wins the game.

The ultimate aim of the Pawn is its promotion. Every success which brings this consummation nearer, approximately increases its value 100%. As the value increases in this ratio, it increases also the extent of the loss suffered if the Pawn or group of Pawns is captured.

A doubled Pawn arising from capture toward the center is a small evil. Questionable is the doubled Pawn produced by capture away from the center because, as a rule, the adversary gains a preponderance in another sector of the board.

In any case, the doubled Pawn is weak if isolated, and becomes incomparably weaker if it stands on an open file which the adversary can occupy. In a trebled Pawn, the loss of value is obviously much bigger still.

Furthermore, especially in certain endgames, Pawns can practically lose all value through being isolated.

In the following position, Black should resign:

Even without the Bishop Pawn—or without the Rook Pawn
—resistance would be out of the question. But take away the
Knight Pawn and the game, if correctly played, should end in
a draw! So we see that the removal of a Pawn, in this position,
was in itself quite unimportant; it was the resulting isolation
of the two remaining Pawns that left them entirely devalued.

This short disquisition merely reminds us of already known
facts. But these facts are of the utmost importance in assess-
ing sacrificial combinations of all kinds: the Pawns are the
steel structure of every position and ordinarily dictate the
course of events.

To the experienced player, this truth has become part of
himself, so much so that he will detect the strength or weakness of a Pawn formation quite automatically and marshal his
thoughts and make his decisions accordingly. He will not
hesitate to give up a wing Pawn for some advance in development; but on the other hand, he will think twice before sacrificing a center Pawn. He will give up a Pawn with a light
heart, if he thereby destroys the hostile Pawn formation; and
rather than see his own Pawns devalued, he will frequently
prefer to surrender a Pawn.

In this way, business is often combined with pleasure, as, for
instance, when a choice has to be made between defending a
doubtful Pawn formation while maintaining the material bal-

ance, or launching an attack by means of a small sacrifice. In the latter case, the original attacker who has speculated on the weakness of the adverse Pawn position can, at times, experience the bitterest disappointment.

The appraisal of Pawn formations must take account of the development and placement of the pieces. Where the pieces are well-placed—sometimes, as we have seen, as the result of sacrifices—a poor Pawn formation can generally be endured with good grace. On the contrary, when the pieces are unfavorably situated, the slightest Pawn weakness can become fatal.

The disposition of the Pawns must also be allowed for, when prospective sacrifices are being assessed. This is particularly the case where the attacker expects partial or even full compensation in Pawns.

We often read notes to this effect: "The attacker has two Pawns and the attack for his piece; the sacrifice was therefore sound." But it is by no means a matter of indifference which particular Pawns are involved. Are they sound or sickly, united or isolated, active or in reserve, passed or otherwise? These questions are vital. The respective answers will enlighten us as to the size of the real sacrifice and its likelihood of success.

If compensation is looked for, it must be represented by valuable Pawns or the object will not be attained. It will usually be necessary for the compensating Pawns to participate in some way in the attack. It is the attack that always remains the first consideration.

The formula that three Pawns are the equivalent of a piece must be taken with circumspection. In the endgame it is frequently true, in the middle game only in certain circumstances: there must at least be some prospects of attack. This is the more important as the adversary may conceivably be in a position to bring the weight of his extra piece to bear in the scales.

All other things being equal, the extra piece should usually be stronger than the three Pawns, and in defensive positions it frequently happens that even four healthy Pawns are not a sufficient compensation for the piece.

A variation of the Evans Gambit Declined illustrates the point:

	WHITE	BLACK		WHITE	BLACK
1	P-K4	P-K4	6	NxP	N-R3
2	N-KB3	N-QB3	7	P-Q4	P-Q3
3	B-B4	B-B4	8	BxN	PxN
4	P-QN4	B-N3	9	BxP	KR-N1
5	P-N5	N-R4	10	BxPch	KxB
			11	BxP	Q-N4

White is the proud owner of four Pawns of which two are handsome center Pawns, and yet stands to lose. The second player's superior development and the weakness evoked on White's Queen-side by the advance P-QN4-5, have a decisive effect. It is not in our province to analyze this position. But if you examine it, you will find after a few tries that White is almost defenseless as soon as the hostile attack gets going.

Finally, let it be noted that as a rule, Pawns provide a better compensation for a Knight than for a Bishop. A Bishop is far better equipped for the struggle against passed Pawns, so much so that it can frequently challenge three sound passed Pawns successfully. Offhand I can recall three modern examples (Davidson-Vidmar, Semmering, 1926; Colle-Vidmar, Carlsbad, 1929; and Vidmar-Stoltz, Bled, 1931), all of which came to an ending where a Bishop prevailed against three sound Pawns.

If, for any reason, the attacker makes an unusually heavy sacrifice (a Rook, say, or two minor pieces), the question of Pawn compensation loses in importance. In normal circumstances, Pawns may offer compensation for a minor piece, but not for a Rook, let alone two minor pieces. The reason is that in such cases the Pawns would be numerous and that this would be of problematical value. After all, only one or two of these Pawns would have queening prospects.

When going in for such large stakes, the attacker should not rely on an equivalent in Pawns; at the most, he can see in them a pleasing concomitant. An exception must naturally be made in those cases where the attacker obtains by force a number of well-advanced Pawns (usually two united passed Pawns).

The whole subject is very extensive, and closely connected with positional play. It can therefore only be touched upon within the framework of a treatise on the nature of sacrifices. Nevertheless, familiarity with the subject is essential for the proper judgment of sacrifices and combinations. Only on this basis can the real value of each unit be recognized and a convincing answer be given to the question of the actual size of a real sacrifice.

Sacrifices of a Pawn, a minor piece, a Rook and also of two pieces have already been discussed. The sacrifice of the exchange and of the Queen are, for certain reasons, to be treated at length in the two following chapters.

THE EXCHANGE SACRIFICE

All chess units have, in the language of the stock exchange, two prices, the par value and the quoted rate. The par value represents the *absolute*, the price from day to day the *relative* values.

The absolute value forms the basis on which exchanges are made; the relative value is the decisive factor for positional play, for combinations and especially for sacrifices. The simpler the position, the more the absolute value carries weight. The more complicated the position, the more does the relative value gain in importance. In the original position, the absolute value practically counts alone, the relative value only arises in the course of the game. The lead is given by the absolute value, for it is enduring as against the relative value, which is variable and transient. The permanent value expresses in an unequivocal manner the comparative power of the various units.

If, however, we examine the scale of absolute values, we find an extraordinary circumstance: there is one value which is determined with mathematical exactitude, but which, in chess can never be realized from the point of view of material. And that is the "Exchange."

We know that Knight and Bishop, Queen and two Rooks, two Rooks and three pieces, are equivalent; and further, that three sound Pawns are approximately equal to a piece.

In normal circumstances, all exchanges of units are made on

this basis. For the "exchange" and the difference in value between a Rook and a minor piece, we have no absolute equivalent. As two Rooks are equal to three minor pieces and a minor piece equals three good Pawns, the Rook should be exactly equal to a minor piece and a half, or to one minor piece and a Pawn and a half. But there are no half-pieces or half-Pawns. There can never be an exact *quid pro quo* in this case: the counter-value must always be either bigger or smaller. You either "win" or "lose" the "exchange."

It follows that an exactly even transaction will only be possible in certain circumstances and will arise on the basis of the practically unlimited scale of relative values.

One consequence of this peculiarity of the "exchange" is that in capturing two minor pieces for a Rook and two Pawns or a Queen for a Rook, minor piece and Pawns, there can also be no exact *quid pro quo*. In the first case, a Rook and one and a half Pawns are required; in the second, a Rook, minor piece and one and a half Pawns. Thus these exchanges are also dependent on specific positional and combinative factors.

The generally accepted standpoint, which also obtains in this book, is that any voluntary loss in material counts as a sacrifice. We must therefore speak of a sacrifice of the "exchange" where a Rook is given up for a minor piece and a Pawn. But the formula "gives up the 'exchange' for two Pawns" is incorrect; it should be "wins two Pawns for the 'exchange.'"

As to type, the sacrifice of the exchange can serve any purpose we have discussed previously. It can be a sacrifice for development, or an obstructive, or King's Field sacrifice, etc. In the main, it will strive for an improvement in the position of the minor pieces and must be considered in that case a special kind of sacrifice. The following examples will supply more detailed data.

EXAMPLE 33

Ruy Lopez
Teplitz-Schönau, 1922

WHITE	BLACK	WHITE	BLACK
Dr. K. Treybal	R. Spielmann	Dr. K. Treybal	R. Spielmann
1 P-K4	P-K4	7 B-N3	P-Q4
2 N-KB3	N-QB3	8 PxP	B-K3
3 B-N5	P-QR3	9 P-B3	B-K2
4 B-R4	N-B3	10 B-K3	O-O
5 O-O	NxP	11 QN-Q2	P-B4
6 P-Q4	P-QN4	12 NxN	....

Leads to very sharp play. 12 PxP e.p. is also good, but 12 N-Q4 is probably best.

12	BPxN	13 N-Q4	NxN
		14 PxN	....

White now has the familiar pressure on the open Queen Bishop file against Black's backward Pawn. But his prospects are problematical. He lacks the minor piece best suited for occupying QB5: a Knight. The Queen Bishop cannot reach QB5 in any foreseeable time.

14	P-QR4!	15 P-QR4	P-B3!
		16 P-B4	Q-Q2

White threatened 17 P-KN4.

17   PxP   ....

The beginning of an ingenious, but not wholly unobjectionable, enterprise against Black's center.

17 ....   PxP   18 P-N4   P-R5!

Winning an important tempo. The Bishop must give way, as 19 P-B5, PxB is in Black's favor.

19 B-R2   BxP

Objectively, 19 . . . P-N3, threatening . . . P-N5-N6, may have been even better. But I hoped that my opponent would play for the win of the exchange—and my expectations were fulfilled.

20 BxPch   K-R1!

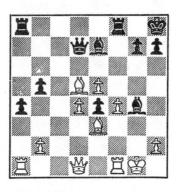

21 P-K6?   ....

White plays as I anticipated. A better way of preventing the loss of a piece is 21 B-B6! In that case, I intended to continue with 21 . . . Q-B1; 22 B-N7 (22 Q-B2 is unfavorable because of 22 . . . B-B6! when White must give up the exchange, but is still exposed to a strong attack), QxB; 23 QxB, P-N5 and estimated that my mobile majority on the Queen-side would outweigh the as yet immobile hostile center—which is probably correct.

The text move affords Black an opportunity for a decisive sacrifice of the exchange.

21   ....   BxP

There was another winning line, namely the simple 21 . . . QxB; 22 QxB, R-B4! (not 22 . . . Q-KB4?, which favors White: 23 QxQ, RxQ; 24 QR-B1 etc.) and White loses the King Pawn without any compensation, which is all the more unpleasant as after 23 QR-B1, QxKP, the loss of White's Queen is already threatened by 24 . . . R-N4! Against passive waiting moves on White's part, Black even has time for . . . R-R3 and . . . RxKP.

The move in the text is certainly no weaker, but it is more in accordance with my style. Black keeps Bishop and Pawn against Rook, but incidentally he has the two Bishops—a most weighty consideration.

The principle that two Bishops and a Rook are as strong as two Rooks and a Knight has already been established by Dr. Tarrasch. This principle can be extended to cases where an inactive Bishop is on the side of the Rooks. Such a situation obtains here, where White's Bishop at K3 is seriously obstructed by his own Pawns at Q4 and KB4. To this have to be added advantages in the Pawn position: Black not only has an extra Pawn, but also a passed Pawn at K5 and a menacing majority on the Queen-side. If we also consider that White's King position is torn up and that the two Bishops are particularly fitted both to initiate attacks and to support advancing Pawns, it follows that the text move offers quite a number of important advantages.

Nevertheless, I do not maintain that this course is better than the straight path, which consisted in the guileless capture at Q4. It is a matter of taste.

Finally, I must remark that this game is intended less to present a "brilliant combination" than to illustrate the relative values of two Rooks and a weak minor piece against Rook, two Bishops and a strong Pawn. We shall see that the side which is superior in material, is quite helpless.

| 22 | BxR | RxB | 23 | Q-B2 | B-B5! |

In order to reply to 24 QxKP with 24 . . . B-Q4 followed by 25 . . . Q-N5ch.

24	R-B2	B-Q6	27	R-N2	Q-N2
25	Q-Q2	P-N5	28	P-B5	P-R6
26	K-R1	P-N6!	29	P-B6	BxP
			30	RxRP	RxR

As a rule it is very dangerous for the materially weaker side to exchange the remaining Rook. But when in possession of two Bishops, the transaction becomes much more plausible. Here the question no longer really matters, as Black obtains a far-advanced passed Pawn on the Queen-side. This points to a quick decision.

| 31 | PxR | B-B7! |

Threatens . . . P-N7 etc.

| 32 | R-N1 | Q-B1 | 33 | P-QR4 | . . . . |

33 Q-B1 is met by 33 . . . Q-B6!

| 33 | . . . . | Q-KB4 |

Black menaces the White King and at the same time prepares the advance of the Knight Pawn. The immediate 33 . . . P-N7? is answered by 34 Q-N4!

34 P-R5	Q-B6ch	35 R-N2	P-R4

Creating a loophole for his own King and also menacing
. . . P-R5-R6. If White tries 36 P-R6, the Pawn goes lost by
36 . . . Q-B8ch etc.

36 K-N1	P-N7!

White resigns, for if 37 QxB, QxBch followed by
38 . . . Q-B8ch etc.

From the foregoing game, we can draw the following
conclusions:

If a player, after sacrificing the exchange, remains with Rook,
two Bishops and a sound extra Pawn against two Rooks and
minor piece, and the position is otherwise approximately even,
then his material disadvantage, which can only be expressed
theoretically and amounts to half a Pawn, becomes a trifling
matter.

The material minus is balanced by the dynamic plus, so that
the chances are fairly evenly distributed. Obviously the two
Bishops cannot be counted as an asset where the adversary has
them too.

As the sacrificing side remains with at least three pieces
(Rook and two Bishops), the opponent must have at least two
Rooks and a minor piece. It is this latter piece which tips the
scale. If well-posted, it will achieve the minimum goal of getting itself exchanged for one of the Bishops, *whereupon the
dynamic advantage will disappear.* In this connection, the likelihood of exchange is greater when the opposing minor piece
is a Bishop rather than a Knight.

Another controlling factor is the extra Pawn, for the prospects of either player vary in proportion to this Pawn's strength
or weakness.

The state of the files also plays a role here. If only one line is open for the Rooks, the opposing Bishops are generally in a position to permanently prevent the Rooks from penetrating into the other player's position. Where there are several open files available, one has to reckon with unusually effective play by the Rooks. In this latter case, then—unless there is some special incentive—the sacrifice of the exchange is better avoided.

On the other hand, this sacrifice can be undertaken without a qualm in restricted or locked positions, for the Rooks are unwieldy in such situations. The risk will not be great even without the two Bishops and the extra Pawn: the required dynamic advantage arises out of the decreased usefulness of the Rooks. Where the sacrifice is combined with positional advantages—weakness, for example, in the hostile Pawn formation—or with prospects of attack, it will always have to be assessed favorably.

The sacrifice of the exchange for two Bishops and a Pawn is often useful for defensive purposes. But I must refrain from doing more than to point to a model game: Maroczy-Rubinstein, Carlsbad, 1907.

The student should not shrink from these rather numerous stipulations. With a little practice, he will soon be able to grasp all these circumstances instinctively as and when they arise. He will acquire what in chess parlance is termed sound positional judgment.

EXAMPLE 34

King's Gambit Declined
Carlsbad, 1923

WHITE	BLACK	WHITE	BLACK
R. Spielmann	Dr. S. Tarrasch	R. Spielmann	Dr. S. Tarrasch
1 P-K4	P-K4	3 N-KB3	P-Q3
2 P-KB4	B-B4	4 P-B3	B-KN5

[To counteract the effect of this pin, White now has recourse to a line originated by Marshall.]

| 5 | PxP | PxP | 7 | Q-B2 | N-QB3 |
| 6 | Q-R4ch | B-Q2 | 8 | P-QN4 | B-Q3 |

Necessary, else 9 P-N5 wins the King Pawn.

| 9 | B-B4 | N-B3 | 11 | O-O | N-N3 |
| 10 | P-Q3 | N-K2 | 12 | B-K3 | .... |

12 P-QR4! is stronger than the text, which permits Black to obtain counterplay.

| 12 | .... | P-N4! | 14 | P-QR3! | PxP |
| 13 | B-N3 | P-QR4 | 15 | BPxP | .... |

15 ....   O-O

Black's Queen-side advance has succeeded in forcing 15 BPxP with a consequent weakening of White's center. But more could not be achieved. The gain of a Pawn by 15 . . . BxP? is refuted by 16 N-N5!, O-O; 17 NxBP, RxN; 18 BxRch, KxB; 19 Q-N3ch and 20 QxB.

| 16 | N-B3 | P-B3 | 17 | P-R3 | Q-K2 |
| | | | 18 | N-K2 | B-N1 |

He intends to exchange Bishops after . . . B-R2 in the hope of establishing a Knight at KB5. The procedure is somewhat labored. The immediate 18 . . . N-R4 is simpler.

19	K-R2	B-R2	22	KN-Q4	Q-Q3
20	B-N5	P-R3	23	N-B5	BxN
21	BxN	QxB	24	RxB	N-B5
			25	R-KB1	....

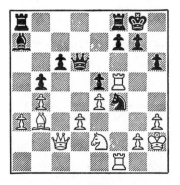

Up to this point Black has defended himself ably and picked up some positional advantages in the process. He has the better Pawn formation, as White's Pawns at QR3 and Q3 are backward and may become weak. As against this, White has built up strong pressure on the King Bishop file, which circumstance the second player seems to underestimate.

25 ....   P-N3?

It would be better to decline White's offer of the exchange implied by 25 R-KB1. For this purpose there is no alternative but to play 25 . . . N-K3! If then 26 Q-R2 (threatening 27 RxBP and 28 BxN), Black plays 26 . . . QR-K1, threatening on his part to free himself with 27 . . . P-B3 and 28 . . . K-R1, followed by an attack on White's Pawn weaknesses.

The text move "wins" the exchange at the cost of enabling White's attack, hitherto directed only against KB7, to spread over the whole King-side.

26	R/B1xN	KPxR	27	P-K5!	Q-K2
			28	R-B6!	....

The powerful establishment of the Rook on this square is the point of the sacrifice. There are now many threats, above all 29 P-Q4 and only then capture at KN6 by Rook or Queen.

If Black plays 28 . . . QxKP there follows 29 RxPch, K-R2; 30 P-Q4, after which 30 . . . QxN is forced. True, Black remains with two Rooks for the Queen, but his King-side is so critically weakened that successful defense is, in the long run, impossible. Yet this would be better than the defense which Black actually selects.

28 .... K-N2

If 28 . . . K-R1; 29 Q-B3 looks very strong in view of the threat of 30 P-K6 etc. But Black replies 30 . . . K-R2, leaving White's Queen rather ineffectual at QB3.

Hence 28 . . . K-R1 is best answered in the manner of the text.

29 P-Q4 BxP

Despair. Of course, White cannot capture the Bishop at once because of 30 . . . QxKP, whereby he regains the piece under favorable conditions. But White has a different method, which is decisive.

However, Black's position is untenable in any event. Thus 29 . . . QR-Q1 is answered simply by 30 Q-K4. White first confiscates the King Bishop Pawn and then storms the King's position with P-KR4 etc.

30 BxP! BxP?

He should play 30 . . . RxB; 31 QxPch, K-B1—though Black still has a lost game after 32 NxB, RxR; 33 PxR, Q-KB2; 34 QxPch, K-K1; 35 QxP (if 35 . . . RxP?; 36 Q-N8ch etc.).

But after the text move, there is a mate in two.

31 QxPch Resigns

In this instance, the sacrifice of the exchange considerably enhanced the efficacy of all of White's pieces—above all assuring a commanding position for his remaining Rook. This is typical of the exchange sacrifice, and similar cases occur frequently. One more reason why a separate chapter is devoted to this type of sacrifice.

EXAMPLE 35

Caro-Kann Defense
Munich, 1909

WHITE	BLACK	WHITE	BLACK
	Dr. S.		Dr. S.
R. Spielmann	Tartakover	R. Spielmann	Tartakover
1 P-K4	P-QB3	3 N-QB3	PxP
2 P-Q4	P-Q4	4 NxP	N-B3
		5 N-N3	. . . .

The treatment initiated by the text move was subsequently adopted by Alekhine.

| 5 . . . | P-K4 | 6 N-B3 | . . . . |

With the move in the text, White obtains a noticeable lead in development.

| 6 . . . | PxP | 7 NxP | B-QB4 |
| | | 8 B-K3 | . . . . |

Only much later did I realize that this is not the right continuation. White must play 8 Q-K2ch! and if 8 . . . Q-K2; 9 QxQch followed by 10 N/Q4-B5—or if 8 . . . B-K2; 9 B-K3 and 10 O-O-O—with advantage to White in either case.

| 8 . . . | Q-N3 | 9 Q-K2 | . . . . |

By indirectly guarding both QN2 and Q4, this move makes Queen-side castling possible.

9 ....   O-O   10 O-O-O   N-Q4?

A serious infraction of the rules of development. After
10 ... R-K1; 11 Q-Q2, B-KN5; 12 P-KB3 (sounder is
12 B-K2), B-K3; 13 B-KN5, BxN; 14 QxB, QN-Q2 Black has
the better game.

11 Q-R5   N-B3

Nor can the damage be repaired by either 11 ... N-Q2
(with a view to ... QN-B3) or 11 ... NxB. Because of the
strong position of the White Queen, which was enabled to
reach the King-side by the ill-advised 10 ... N-Q4?, Black's
King's Field remains in grave danger.

12 Q-R4   B-KN5

Black's last move was well thought out.

If White replies 13 B-K2, Black's answer is 13 ... BxB and
the White King Bishop, which is important for the attack, is
eliminated; if the threatened Rook moves, Black has gained the
necessary tempo for developing his Queen Knight; finally, if
13 P-KB3, the chief point of Black's last move becomes manifest: he plays 13 ... B-K3, and, as the White Bishop on K3
is no longer guarded, the otherwise strong 14 N/N3-B5 is refuted by 14 ... BxN/B4 etc.

But, however fine Tartakover's idea is, the damage wrought by 10 . . . N-Q4? cannot be undone. White's reply cuts across the second player's calculations.

13 B-Q3!   BxR   14 RxB   . . . .

We have here a full sacrifice of the exchange, with the single-minded idea of promoting White's development. White has no material compensation, though he does have the two Bishops. Besides, almost all his forces point menacingly to the Black King.

The acceptance of the exchange sacrifice was virtually compulsory, as 13 B-Q3! threatened 14 BxPch; and the loss of time involved in retreating 13 . . . B-K3 would be even less bearable than acceptance of the offer.

14 . . . .   QN-Q2   15 N/N3-B5   N-K4?

This further mistake by Black leads to his immediate downfall. Essential was 15 . . . K-R1, when White can continue the attack by 16 P-KN4, P-KN3; 17 P-N5, N-KN1; 18 R-N1 threatening R-N3-R3.

The text move is an additional instance of the observation that after a sacrifice, the defender's power of resistance declines not only objectively, but subjectively as well.

16 NxNP!   . . . .

A mating sacrifice which cannot be accepted: 16 . . . KxN; 17 Q-N5ch, N-N3; 18 N-B5ch, K-N1; 19 QxN with unavoidable mate.

The refusal, however, also leads to a hopeless game. Black loses only a Pawn, but one that is of greater value than a piece!

16 . . . .   Q-Q1   17 N/N7-B5   . . . .

This position deserves examination.

In a material sense, the same kind of position arose in the preceding game (Example 34). But the Pawns play a different

role here. What counts here is not the *extra* White Pawn, but the *missing* Black Pawn!

So we can recognize a positive and negative significance in Pawn formations. It would lead us too far afield to go into this question more thoroughly. Generally speaking, it can be stated that in those positions where the active cooperation of the Pawns is required, the material aspect (the extra Pawn) acquires added importance. Where it is a case of creating a weakness in the enemy camp by the elimination of one of his Pawns, the question of material gain (win of a Pawn) is a secondary consideration.

Applied to the present position, this proposition can be stated specifically: the gain of the King Knight Pawn was in itself unimportant. What mattered was the resulting weakness in Black's position—a weakness that was worth producing even at the cost of a sacrifice.

17	....	N-N3	20	PxB	Q-B3
18	Q-R6	N-K1	21	N-N5	Q-R1
19	N-B3!	BxBch	22	N-K7ch	Resigns

Mate in two follows.

So much for the sacrifice of the exchange.

A sacrifice in value of a different kind is that of two minor pieces for a Rook, or for a Rook and Pawn. We have seen an instance of this (Example 13) in the chapter on obstructive sacrifices. The broad general rules for this type of sacrifice have been set forth in the previous chapter.

This sacrifice is of the same size as that of the exchange sacrifice: one and a half Pawns. The object is, naturally, to obtain suddenly increased action by the Rooks or at least one Rook.

In the middle game, this maneuver will generally assist in a King-side attack. In the endgame, it tends more often to help in the capture of enemy Pawns or in escorting one's own passed Pawns.

The sacrifice will be particularly effective if the two minor pieces are left, without the assistance of a Rook. If the two minor pieces are Bishops, the sacrifice will only be possible in exceptional cases. Against Bishop and Knight, or against two Knights, the sacrifice will nearly always succeed.

One brief example from my literary practice may prove illuminating. In revising Collijn's *Laröbok i Schack* in Stockholm in 1919, I came across the following variation in an old textbook:

	WHITE	BLACK		WHITE	BLACK
1	P-K4	P-K4	11	PxB	PxP
2	N-KB3	N-QB3	12	PxP	QxBP
3	B-B4	B-B4	13	N-Q2	Q-R6
4	O-O	P-Q3	14	Q-B8	N-B3
5	P-B3	B-KN5	15	QxR	N-KN5
6	P-Q4	PxP	16	QxPch	N-K2
7	Q-N3	Q-Q2	17	N-B3	QxN
8	BxPch	QxB	18	B-K3	NxB
9	QxP	K-Q2	19	Q-N3	QxQch
10	QxR	BxN	20	RPxQ	NxR
			21	KxN	....

[*See diagram on page 185.*]

This position, the evolution of which will not be discussed here, was given as in Black's favor. I am, however, of a different opinion and in the *Larobok* I appraised the position as being in White's favor. Why? The Black King Rook Pawn is isolated and will have to be looked after permanently, thus throwing the second player on the defensive. This suffices to make the Rook most effective and to counterbalance the slight material odds (half a Pawn).

Such is my conviction, though other masters may not share my views. There are things in chess which cannot be proved by single examples and which can only be assessed on the basis of many years' experience. An exhaustive analysis of the example given, would therefore be neither desirable nor convincing. I only give it as an illustration of my way of thinking.

THE QUEEN SACRIFICE

The real sacrifice of the Queen is always a partial sacrifice. The loss of the Queen is offset largely by other material—but not in full. The compensation is usually a Rook and a minor piece and, perhaps, a Pawn. If two Pawns are obtained, the term "sacrifice" is not applicable; the correct terminology, in that case, is: "wins Rook, minor piece and two Pawns for the Queen."

According to our scale of values, the material sacrificed usually amounts to a Pawn and a half, which in this respect is equivalent to the sacrifice of the exchange.

Without wishing to rebel against a good old custom, I do think that it would be desirable to give all such sacrifices a common name where the size can only be expressed in mathematical terms as it amounts to half a piece or half a Pawn. A suitable term would be "sacrificing the exchange," which is already current in the case of giving up a Rook for a minor piece.

As this is only a suggestion, I shall refrain from making more definite proposals concerning the differentiation between the various sacrifices in value.

As all that matters from a general point of view has been said, we can pass on to our illustrations.

EXAMPLE 36

King's Gambit Declined
(in effect)
Vienna, 1907

WHITE	BLACK	WHITE	BLACK
R. Spielmann	G. Maroczy	R. Spielmann	G. Maroczy
1 P-K4	P-K4	4 P-Q3	N-KB3
2 N-QB3	B-B4	5 P-B4	B-KN5
3 B-B4	P-Q3	6 N-B3	N-B3
		7 N-QR4	N-Q2

Black's treatment of the defense is similar to Schlechter's in Example 2. But the line of play favors White.

8 NxB	PxN	9 O-O	PxP
		10 BxP	....

10 ....   N/B3-K4?

The second player's position was not exactly inviting, but with 10 . . . O-O and possibly . . . B-K3 later on, it was still tenable. The text move permits a very strong Queen sacrifice.

10 . . . N/Q2-K4? is also answered by the Queen sacrifice, with the possible continuation 11 NxN!, Q-Q5ch; 12 K-R1, BxQ; 13 BxPch—after which Black's King has to move to B1 with even better prospects for White than in the actual play.

11   NxN!   BxQ

Or 11 . . . NxN; 12 BxN!, BxQ; 13 BxNP! etc.

12   NxP   Q-B3

The Queen makes for the open. At K2 she is worse off, and is exposed to attacks by hostile minor pieces.

13   QRxB   R-KB1   14   BxP   QxP

Let us examine the sacrifice. White has only two Bishops and a Pawn for the Queen. From a dogmatic point of view, the sacrifice amounts to only two Pawns, according to our scale of values. As a practical proposition, the sacrifice is considerably bigger. The calculation that the Queen equals three minor pieces is doubtless correct, but the conversion of one of the minor pieces into three Pawns is only valid under certain reservations and, *ceteris paribus,* the Pawns will fulfill their task only with difficulty. In a contest against the Queen they are almost valueless. The power concentrated in the Queen, namely that of two minor pieces and three Pawns, can be unleashed with incomparably greater rapidity.

We see here the immense advantage of centralized power as against scattered forces. This advantage already obtains in the struggle of minor pieces against Pawns; as between major pieces and Pawns, this factor is generally decisive.

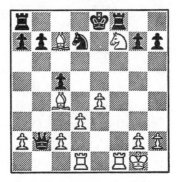

In certain circumstances this state of affairs may be reversed, namely, when the sacrificing side has the attack and one of the compensating Pawns can intervene directly—say a passed Pawn which advances menacingly, or a well-advanced Pawn giving its own aggressively posted pieces strong support. Such an exceptional case arises here.

15   R-B2?   . . . .

This is in contradiction to the foregoing discussion, and is a mistake which helps the adversary to his feet.

Had I possessed, in those days, the experience which I have today, the theoretically correct move 15 P-K5! (immediate utilization of the compensating Pawn!) would not have escaped me. Even a superficial examination shows that White's attack gains enormously in strength thereby and will no doubt become irresistible. Above all there threatens 16 P-K6, N-B3; 17 N-Q6ch, K-K2; 18 N-B5ch, K-K1; 19 NxPch, K-K2; 20 N-B5ch, K-K1; 21 B-N5ch!, QxB; 22 N-Q6ch and 23 NxQ etc. There are, besides, many other threats which the attentive reader can easily find for himself.

After the faulty move in the text, White gradually drifts into an inferior position and should lose. But Black also plays weakly and gets a lost game, escaping with a draw after a further mistake by White. This part of the game has no inner relation to the Queen sacrifice and is of no importance for our purpose.

15	. . . .	N-B3	22	R/Q3-Q2	Q-N5
16	B-K5	Q-N3	23	P-QR3	QxP
17	N-Q6ch	K-Q2	24	PxP	Q-K6ch
18	P-Q4	N-N5	25	K-R1	NxB?
19	KR-Q2	Q-N5	26	N-B5 dis ch	QxR
20	P-B3	QxP	27	RxQch	K-B2
21	R-Q3	Q-N7	28	B-Q5	QR-Q1?

He should play 28 . . . P-KN3!

29	P-R3	R-Q2		35	R-N6	R-B3
30	N-Q4	R-B8ch		36	RxPch	K-N2
31	K-R2	P-QR3		37	R-N6ch	K-R2
32	R-N2	N-B3		38	P-K5	R-R3
33	N-K6ch	K-B1		39	R-Q6!	R-K2
34	BxN	PxB		40	N-Q4?	....

40 N-Q8! wins for White.

40	....	K-N2!		43	NxR	PxN
41	P-B6ch	K-B2		44	RxP	R-K2
42	N-B5	RxP			Drawn	

EXAMPLE 37

King's Gambit
Gothenburg, 1920

WHITE	BLACK		WHITE	BLACK
R. Spielmann	J. Möller		R. Spielmann	J. Möller
1 P-K4	P-K4		4 P-B3	N-B3
2 P-KB4	PxP		5 P-Q4	P-Q4
3 Q-B3	N-QB3		6 P-K5	N-K5
			7 B-N5	....

An attempt to avoid theoretically known paths, as the usual continuation 7 BxP, B-K2 followed by 8 . . . O-O and 9 . . . P-B3 favors Black.

7 ....   Q-R5ch

Black takes up the challenge; he can also continue his development with 7 . . . B-K2 etc.

8 K-B1   P-N4

The second player now threatens to win with 9 . . . B-KN5.

This is more dangerous than the immediate 8 . . . N-N6ch; 9 PxN, QxR; 10 PxP, after which White has fine attacking chances for the lost exchange. In playing 7 B-N5, I had counted principally on this variation.

The text move sets the first player new problems. 9 P-KN3 is not feasible because of 9 . . . PxP; 10 PxP, QxR! followed by . . . NxPch etc. Other defensive moves, such as 9 Q-K2, yield up the attack to the opponent, which, in this position, is fatal for White. The following surprising sacrifice of the Queen is the only continuation which promises success.

9   N-Q2!   B-KN5

"Wins" the Queen. Black can decline the offer with 9 . . . B-KB4. Then follows 10 B-Q3 and the dangerous Knight is eliminated. It is a moot point whether White can remain untroubled in the face of the loss of the exchange after 10 B-Q3, N-N6ch; 11 PxN, BxBch; 12 QxB, QxR; 13 PxP, PxP followed by . . . O-O-O etc.

At all events, Black should select this line of play, but the capture of the Queen is tempting, all the more so since Black already has an extra Pawn.

| 10 | NxN | BxQ | 12 | N-B6ch | K-Q1 |
| 11 | NxB | Q-R3 | 13 | P-KR4! | . . . . |

The point. Black certainly has the Queen for only Knight and Bishop, but the move in the text completely shatters his Pawn formation, so that he cannot avoid the loss of several Pawns. In the sequel, Black's pieces become completely insecure, while White's forces gain proportionately in efficiency. White's pieces will find points of attack and act in concert; not so the Black forces. White's King is safe, Black's King will only find a refuge by means of elaborate maneuvers.

Finally, the Black Queen, thanks to the inflexible firmness of White's Pawn formation, will not find a worthy occupation for a long time to come and will have to be thankful to escape unscathed from the attentions of her tormentors, the White minor pieces.

On these grounds I decided to sacrifice. As the sequel shows, this appraisal was correct. In accordance with the points cited above, White retains excellent attacking chances, while Black does not succeed in evolving a useful plan. The fact that a sacrifice frequently causes planlessness and confusion in the opponent's game, is confirmed in this instance also.

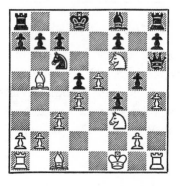

13   ....   B-K2

The alternative is 13 ... N-K2, in order to preserve the center Pawn. But then too, Black's position is one of great difficulty, as White can for example play 14 B-Q3, putting Black's Queen in a position of serious jeopardy.

In such positions, analysis is impracticable because of the wide ramification of possibilities: examination leads into too many byways. This enhances the attacker's prospects in over-the-board play, as he can always reckon with the probability that his adversary will not consistently hit on the strongest move.

14	NxNP	Q-N3	15	NxQP	BxN
			16	PxB	Q-B7?

The Queen is badly placed here and is in danger of being trapped. 16 . . . QxP is better, even though White then keeps the upper hand. He plays 17 NxKBP! (not 17 BxP, Q-B4, after which the threat of 18 . . . N-K2 is troublesome). This also wins a tempo by the threat of 18 N-K6ch and has, in addition, the advantage that 17 . . . Q-B4 can be answered neatly by 18 B-Q3.

The spurned Pawn soon develops a very strong blockading effect.

17	B-K2	N-K2	18	NxKBP	. . . .

With two Bishops and two strong compensating Pawns ready for instant action, White has almost attained material equality.

18	. . . .	P-QB4?

Black is entirely undeveloped, with King and Queen very badly placed, and with bad Pawn weaknesses on the King-side. Further, he is threatened with a powerful hostile advance. The last thing Black should attempt, is opening up lines. Worse yet, the text move frees one of the most dangerous hostile Pawns.

Consequently 18 . . . P-QB3, followed by 19 . . . K-B2, is in order.

19	R-R3!	PxP?

The decisive mistake. The Queen should retreat, preferably to B4. Black's game, however, is already very bad: 19 . . . Q-B4; 20 R-B3, PxP; 21 PxP, R-QB1; 22 B-Q3, Q-N5; 23 N-K2 etc.

20   R-Q3!   . . . .

And so Black's Queen is trapped! 21 B-Q1 is threatened, and the only flight possibility, 20 . . . Q-R5, is refuted by 21 RxPch.

20	. . . .	K-Q2	22	NxQ	PxP
21	B-Q1	QxRch	23	PxP	. . . .

With the advantage of two Bishops and a Pawn against a Rook and with the superior position as well, White now has an easily won game.

23	. . . .	QR-Q1	24	B-K2	N-B4
			25	B-B4	K-B2

Hastens his downfall.

26	R-N1	P-N3	27	P-K6 dis ch	K-B1
			28	N-K5	Resigns

We can refrain from giving further illustrations. In the *real* Queen sacrifice, the minimum compensation which has to be looked for, should comprise two minor pieces and two Pawns. Where the *quid pro quo* is smaller, the sacrifice, if sound, is necessarily a *sham* sacrifice. Where the compensation is bigger, say three minor pieces or two Rooks, the transaction cannot be termed a sacrifice, but rather a favorable exchange or even a gain of material.

Not unlike the sacrifice of the exchange, the Queen sacrifice has its own characteristics, based on material circumstances, and cannot be classified as a matter of course with other types.

The two examples given, show a certain similarity with the preventive sacrifice: in both cases, the sacrificial point lies in the center; the opponent is prevented from castling; the King is held fast in the center; co-ordination between the Rooks is impeded and a decision sought before the hostile army can recover. A difference, and at the same time a typical feature of the Queen sacrifice, is the threatened position of the hostile Queen which, together with the King, is exposed to the gravest dangers.

This concludes our review of the Queen sacrifice.

Epilogue

So ENDS THIS FIRST ATTEMPT TO EXPLAIN THE SACRIFICES WHICH occur in practical play, to classify them and to provide them with their own nomenclature. How far I may have succeeded, is left to the judgment of my esteemed readers. It would please me were the critics to take up the subject and to suggest improvements.

The demesne of the sacrifice belongs to the theory of chess and is subject to the same fate as any opening or ending. The theory of chess is the work of the whole chess community. Our theorists are in effect only chroniclers, who collect and give to posterity the ideas of their contemporaries. The individual is as a drop in the ocean.

The present treatise, which discusses a hitherto overlooked chapter of general chess theory, will have to run the gauntlet of the views and suggestions of others, so that gradually, out of the first promptings, a definite structure may grow. I have emphasized on several occasions that this book only expounds my own subjective opinions. It will only be possible to draw objective conclusions from a great number of personal views.

When writing this book, deeply immersed in my subject, I was constantly disturbed by new ideas, new lines of thought, so that it became a matter of difficulty to keep on my intended course.

Unexplored territory is difficult to survey. I myself was frequently surprised at the result of my reflections. For instance, it went against my feelings, nurtured on accepted formulae, to accept unreservedly the conception of the sham sacrifice, including the mating sacrifice as such. But there was nothing for it but to yield to logic.

It has given me much trouble to find appropriate names for the various types of sacrifice. Some of them do not satisfy me even now, in spite of repeated attempts. The hardest was the preventive sacrifice. The name does not convey enough, but I could not find a better one.

Originally I had intended to elucidate sacrifices from other angles. I wanted to speak of sound and unsound sacrifices, of sacrifices for attack and for defense, of strategical and tactical sacrifices, classical and modern sacrifices. But I had to admit to myself that this would have led too far and meant a book twice the size. Also the various categories, at times overlapping, would only have made it more difficult to find one's way; the intended systematizing would ultimately have led to chaos.

A more detailed analysis of the subject may be in order at some future time.

This concludes my treatment of the nature of the sacrifice and I now make way for the critics.

INDEX OF OPENINGS

(The numbers refer to pages)

Alekhine's Defense, 52

Caro-Kann Defense, 21, 27, 64, 180

Danish Gambit Declined, 125

Dutch Defense, 17, 148

French Defense, 36, 70, 119

Giuoco Piano, 104, 114

Grünfeld Defense, 84

King's Gambit, 95, 99, 108, 190

King's Gambit Declined, 14, 176, 187

King's Indian Defense, 59

Queen's Gambit Accepted, 34, 56

Queen's Gambit Declined, 12, 23, 47, 74, 138, 154

Ruy Lopez, 42, 133, 171

Scotch Game, 79

Sicilian Defense, 31

Vienna Game, 91, 129

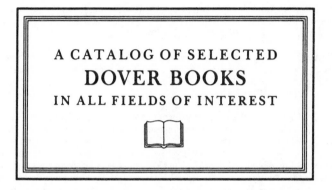

A CATALOG OF SELECTED
DOVER BOOKS
IN ALL FIELDS OF INTEREST

A CATALOG OF SELECTED DOVER
BOOKS IN ALL FIELDS OF INTEREST

CONCERNING THE SPIRITUAL IN ART, Wassily Kandinsky. Pioneering work by father of abstract art. Thoughts on color theory, nature of art. Analysis of earlier masters. 12 illustrations. 80pp. of text. 5⅜ x 8½. 23411-8 Pa. $3.95

ANIMALS: 1,419 Copyright-Free Illustrations of Mammals, Birds, Fish, Insects, etc., Jim Harter (ed.). Clear wood engravings present, in extremely lifelike poses, over 1,000 species of animals. One of the most extensive pictorial sourcebooks of its kind. Captions. Index. 284pp. 9 x 12. 23766-4 Pa. $12.95

CELTIC ART: The Methods of Construction, George Bain. Simple geometric techniques for making Celtic interlacements, spirals, Kells-type initials, animals, humans, etc. Over 500 illustrations. 160pp. 9 x 12. (USO) 22923-8 Pa. $9.95

AN ATLAS OF ANATOMY FOR ARTISTS, Fritz Schider. Most thorough reference work on art anatomy in the world. Hundreds of illustrations, including selections from works by Vesalius, Leonardo, Goya, Ingres, Michelangelo, others. 593 illustrations. 192pp. 7⅛ x 10¼. 20241-0 Pa. $9.95

CELTIC HAND STROKE-BY-STROKE (Irish Half-Uncial from "The Book of Kells"): An Arthur Baker Calligraphy Manual, Arthur Baker. Complete guide to creating each letter of the alphabet in distinctive Celtic manner. Covers hand position, strokes, pens, inks, paper, more. Illustrated. 48pp. 8¼ x 11. 24336-2 Pa. $3.95

EASY ORIGAMI, John Montroll. Charming collection of 32 projects (hat, cup, pelican, piano, swan, many more) specially designed for the novice origami hobbyist. Clearly illustrated easy-to-follow instructions insure that even beginning papercrafters will achieve successful results. 48pp. 8¼ x 11. 27298-2 Pa. $3.50

THE COMPLETE BOOK OF BIRDHOUSE CONSTRUCTION FOR WOODWORKERS, Scott D. Campbell. Detailed instructions, illustrations, tables. Also data on bird habitat and instinct patterns. Bibliography. 3 tables. 63 illustrations in 15 figures. 48pp. 5¼ x 8½. 24407-5 Pa. $2.50

BLOOMINGDALE'S ILLUSTRATED 1886 CATALOG: Fashions, Dry Goods and Housewares, Bloomingdale Brothers. Famed merchants' extremely rare catalog depicting about 1,700 products: clothing, housewares, firearms, dry goods, jewelry, more. Invaluable for dating, identifying vintage items. Also, copyright-free graphics for artists, designers. Co-published with Henry Ford Museum & Greenfield Village. 160pp. 8¼ x 11. 25780-0 Pa. $10.95

HISTORIC COSTUME IN PICTURES, Braun & Schneider. Over 1,450 costumed figures in clearly detailed engravings–from dawn of civilization to end of 19th century. Captions. Many folk costumes. 256pp. 8⅜ x 11¾. 23150-X Pa. $12.95

STICKLEY CRAFTSMAN FURNITURE CATALOGS, Gustav Stickley and L. & J. G. Stickley. Beautiful, functional furniture in two authentic catalogs from 1910. 594 illustrations, including 277 photos, show settles, rockers, armchairs, reclining chairs, bookcases, desks, tables. 183pp. 6½ x 9¼. 23838-5 Pa. $9.95

AMERICAN LOCOMOTIVES IN HISTORIC PHOTOGRAPHS: 1858 to 1949, Ron Ziel (ed.). A rare collection of 126 meticulously detailed official photographs, called "builder portraits," of American locomotives that majestically chronicle the rise of steam locomotive power in America. Introduction. Detailed captions. xi + 129pp. 9 x 12. 27393-8 Pa. $12.95

AMERICA'S LIGHTHOUSES: An Illustrated History, Francis Ross Holland, Jr. Delightfully written, profusely illustrated fact-filled survey of over 200 American lighthouses since 1716. History, anecdotes, technological advances, more. 240pp. 8 x 10¾. 25576-X Pa. $12.95

TOWARDS A NEW ARCHITECTURE, Le Corbusier. Pioneering manifesto by founder of "International School." Technical and aesthetic theories, views of industry, economics, relation of form to function, "mass-production split" and much more. Profusely illustrated. 320pp. 6⅛ x 9¼. (USO) 25023-7 Pa. $9.95

HOW THE OTHER HALF LIVES, Jacob Riis. Famous journalistic record, exposing poverty and degradation of New York slums around 1900, by major social reformer. 100 striking and influential photographs. 233pp. 10 x 7⅞. 22012-5 Pa. $10.95

FRUIT KEY AND TWIG KEY TO TREES AND SHRUBS, William M. Harlow. One of the handiest and most widely used identification aids. Fruit key covers 120 deciduous and evergreen species; twig key 160 deciduous species. Easily used. Over 300 photographs. 126pp. 5⅜ x 8½. 20511-8 Pa. $3.95

COMMON BIRD SONGS, Dr. Donald J. Borror. Songs of 60 most common U.S. birds: robins, sparrows, cardinals, bluejays, finches, more—arranged in order of increasing complexity. Up to 9 variations of songs of each species. Cassette and manual 99911-4 $8.95

ORCHIDS AS HOUSE PLANTS, Rebecca Tyson Northen. Grow cattleyas and many other kinds of orchids—in a window, in a case, or under artificial light. 63 illustrations. 148pp. 5⅜ x 8½. 23261-1 Pa. $4.95

MONSTER MAZES, Dave Phillips. Masterful mazes at four levels of difficulty. Avoid deadly perils and evil creatures to find magical treasures. Solutions for all 32 exciting illustrated puzzles. 48pp. 8¼ x 11. 26005-4 Pa. $2.95

MOZART'S DON GIOVANNI (DOVER OPERA LIBRETTO SERIES), Wolfgang Amadeus Mozart. Introduced and translated by Ellen H. Bleiler. Standard Italian libretto, with complete English translation. Convenient and thoroughly portable—an ideal companion for reading along with a recording or the performance itself. Introduction. List of characters. Plot summary. 121pp. 5¼ x 8½. 24944-1 Pa. $2.95

TECHNICAL MANUAL AND DICTIONARY OF CLASSICAL BALLET, Gail Grant. Defines, explains, comments on steps, movements, poses and concepts. 15-page pictorial section. Basic book for student, viewer. 127pp. 5⅜ x 8½. 21843-0 Pa. $4.95

CATALOG OF DOVER BOOKS

BRASS INSTRUMENTS: Their History and Development, Anthony Baines. Authoritative, updated survey of the evolution of trumpets, trombones, bugles, cornets, French horns, tubas and other brass wind instruments. Over 140 illustrations and 48 music examples. Corrected and updated by author. New preface. Bibliography. 320pp. 5⅜ x 8½. 27574-4 Pa. $9.95

HOLLYWOOD GLAMOR PORTRAITS, John Kobal (ed.). 145 photos from 1926-49. Harlow, Gable, Bogart, Bacall; 94 stars in all. Full background on photographers, technical aspects. 160pp. 8⅜ x 11¼. 23352-9 Pa. $12.95

MAX AND MORITZ, Wilhelm Busch. Great humor classic in both German and English. Also 10 other works: "Cat and Mouse," "Plisch and Plumm," etc. 216pp. 5⅜ x 8½. 20181-3 Pa. $6.95

THE RAVEN AND OTHER FAVORITE POEMS, Edgar Allan Poe. Over 40 of the author's most memorable poems: "The Bells," "Ulalume," "Israfel," "To Helen," "The Conqueror Worm," "Eldorado," "Annabel Lee," many more. Alphabetic lists of titles and first lines. 64pp. 5³⁄₁₆ x 8¼. 26685-0 Pa. $1.00

PERSONAL MEMOIRS OF U. S. GRANT, Ulysses Simpson Grant. Intelligent, deeply moving firsthand account of Civil War campaigns, considered by many the finest military memoirs ever written. Includes letters, historic photographs, maps and more. 528pp. 6⅛ x 9¼. 28587-1 Pa. $11.95

AMULETS AND SUPERSTITIONS, E. A. Wallis Budge. Comprehensive discourse on origin, powers of amulets in many ancient cultures: Arab, Persian Babylonian, Assyrian, Egyptian, Gnostic, Hebrew, Phoenician, Syriac, etc. Covers cross, swastika, crucifix, seals, rings, stones, etc. 584pp. 5⅜ x 8½. 23573-4 Pa. $12.95

RUSSIAN STORIES/PYCCKNE PACCKA3bI: A Dual-Language Book, edited by Gleb Struve. Twelve tales by such masters as Chekhov, Tolstoy, Dostoevsky, Pushkin, others. Excellent word-for-word English translations on facing pages, plus teaching and study aids, Russian/English vocabulary, biographical/critical introductions, more. 416pp. 5⅜ x 8½. 26244-8 Pa. $8.95

PHILADELPHIA THEN AND NOW: 60 Sites Photographed in the Past and Present, Kenneth Finkel and Susan Oyama. Rare photographs of City Hall, Logan Square, Independence Hall, Betsy Ross House, other landmarks juxtaposed with contemporary views. Captures changing face of historic city. Introduction. Captions. 128pp. 8¼ x 11. 25790-8 Pa. $9.95

AIA ARCHITECTURAL GUIDE TO NASSAU AND SUFFOLK COUNTIES, LONG ISLAND, The American Institute of Architects, Long Island Chapter, and the Society for the Preservation of Long Island Antiquities. Comprehensive, well-researched and generously illustrated volume brings to life over three centuries of Long Island's great architectural heritage. More than 240 photographs with authoritative, extensively detailed captions. 176pp. 8¼ x 11. 26946-9 Pa. $14.95

NORTH AMERICAN INDIAN LIFE: Customs and Traditions of 23 Tribes, Elsie Clews Parsons (ed.). 27 fictionalized essays by noted anthropologists examine religion, customs, government, additional facets of life among the Winnebago, Crow, Zuni, Eskimo, other tribes. 480pp. 6⅛ x 9¼. 27377-6 Pa. $10.95

FRANK LLOYD WRIGHT'S HOLLYHOCK HOUSE, Donald Hoffmann. Lavishly illustrated, carefully documented study of one of Wright's most controversial residential designs. Over 120 photographs, floor plans, elevations, etc. Detailed perceptive text by noted Wright scholar. Index. 128pp. 9¼ x 10¾. 27133-1 Pa. $11.95

THE MALE AND FEMALE FIGURE IN MOTION: 60 Classic Photographic Sequences, Eadweard Muybridge. 60 true-action photographs of men and women walking, running, climbing, bending, turning, etc., reproduced from rare 19th-century masterpiece. vi + 121pp. 9 x 12. 24745-7 Pa. $10.95

1001 QUESTIONS ANSWERED ABOUT THE SEASHORE, N. J. Berrill and Jacquelyn Berrill. Queries answered about dolphins, sea snails, sponges, starfish, fishes, shore birds, many others. Covers appearance, breeding, growth, feeding, much more. 305pp. 5¼ x 8¼. 23366-9 Pa. $8.95

GUIDE TO OWL WATCHING IN NORTH AMERICA, Donald S. Heintzelman. Superb guide offers complete data and descriptions of 19 species: barn owl, screech owl, snowy owl, many more. Expert coverage of owl-watching equipment, conservation, migrations and invasions, etc. Guide to observing sites. 84 illustrations. xiii + 193pp. 5⅜ x 8½. 27344-X Pa. $8.95

MEDICINAL AND OTHER USES OF NORTH AMERICAN PLANTS: A Historical Survey with Special Reference to the Eastern Indian Tribes, Charlotte Erichsen-Brown. Chronological historical citations document 500 years of usage of plants, trees, shrubs native to eastern Canada, northeastern U.S. Also complete identifying information. 343 illustrations. 544pp. 6½ x 9¼. 25951-X Pa. $12.95

STORYBOOK MAZES, Dave Phillips. 23 stories and mazes on two-page spreads: Wizard of Oz, Treasure Island, Robin Hood, etc. Solutions. 64pp. 8¼ x 11. 23628-5 Pa. $2.95

NEGRO FOLK MUSIC, U.S.A., Harold Courlander. Noted folklorist's scholarly yet readable analysis of rich and varied musical tradition. Includes authentic versions of over 40 folk songs. Valuable bibliography and discography. xi + 324pp. 5⅜ x 8½. 27350-4 Pa. $9.95

MOVIE-STAR PORTRAITS OF THE FORTIES, John Kobal (ed.). 163 glamor, studio photos of 106 stars of the 1940s: Rita Hayworth, Ava Gardner, Marlon Brando, Clark Gable, many more. 176pp. 8⅜ x 11¼. 23546-7 Pa. $12.95

BENCHLEY LOST AND FOUND, Robert Benchley. Finest humor from early 30s, about pet peeves, child psychologists, post office and others. Mostly unavailable elsewhere. 73 illustrations by Peter Arno and others. 183pp. 5⅜ x 8½. 22410-4 Pa. $6.95

YEKL and THE IMPORTED BRIDEGROOM AND OTHER STORIES OF YIDDISH NEW YORK, Abraham Cahan. Film Hester Street based on Yekl (1896). Novel, other stories among first about Jewish immigrants on N.Y.'s East Side. 240pp. 5⅜ x 8½. 22427-9 Pa. $6.95

SELECTED POEMS, Walt Whitman. Generous sampling from *Leaves of Grass*. Twenty-four poems include "I Hear America Singing," "Song of the Open Road," "I Sing the Body Electric," "When Lilacs Last in the Dooryard Bloom'd," "O Captain! My Captain!"—all reprinted from an authoritative edition. Lists of titles and first lines. 128pp. 5³⁄₁₆ x 8¼. 26878-0 Pa. $1.00

THE BEST TALES OF HOFFMANN, E. T. A. Hoffmann. 10 of Hoffmann's most important stories: "Nutcracker and the King of Mice," "The Golden Flowerpot," etc. 458pp. 5⅜ x 8½. 21793-0 Pa. $9.95

FROM FETISH TO GOD IN ANCIENT EGYPT, E. A. Wallis Budge. Rich detailed survey of Egyptian conception of "God" and gods, magic, cult of animals, Osiris, more. Also, superb English translations of hymns and legends. 240 illustrations. 545pp. 5⅜ x 8½. 25803-3 Pa. $13.95

FRENCH STORIES/CONTES FRANÇAIS: A Dual-Language Book, Wallace Fowlie. Ten stories by French masters, Voltaire to Camus: "Micromegas" by Voltaire; "The Atheist's Mass" by Balzac; "Minuet" by de Maupassant; "The Guest" by Camus, six more. Excellent English translations on facing pages. Also French-English vocabulary list, exercises, more. 352pp. 5⅜ x 8½. 26443-2 Pa. $8.95

CHICAGO AT THE TURN OF THE CENTURY IN PHOTOGRAPHS: 122 Historic Views from the Collections of the Chicago Historical Society, Larry A. Viskochil. Rare large-format prints offer detailed views of City Hall, State Street, the Loop, Hull House, Union Station, many other landmarks, circa 1904-1913. Introduction. Captions. Maps. 144pp. 9⅜ x 12¼. 24656-6 Pa. $12.95

OLD BROOKLYN IN EARLY PHOTOGRAPHS, 1865-1929, William Lee Younger. Luna Park, Gravesend race track, construction of Grand Army Plaza, moving of Hotel Brighton, etc. 157 previously unpublished photographs. 165pp. 8⅞ x 11¾. 23587-4 Pa. $13.95

THE MYTHS OF THE NORTH AMERICAN INDIANS, Lewis Spence. Rich anthology of the myths and legends of the Algonquins, Iroquois, Pawnees and Sioux, prefaced by an extensive historical and ethnological commentary. 36 illustrations. 480pp. 5⅜ x 8½. 25967-6 Pa. $8.95

AN ENCYCLOPEDIA OF BATTLES: Accounts of Over 1,560 Battles from 1479 B.C. to the Present, David Eggenberger. Essential details of every major battle in recorded history from the first battle of Megiddo in 1479 B.C. to Grenada in 1984. List of Battle Maps. New Appendix covering the years 1967-1984. Index. 99 illustrations. 544pp. 6½ x 9¼. 24913-1 Pa. $14.95

SAILING ALONE AROUND THE WORLD, Captain Joshua Slocum. First man to sail around the world, alone, in small boat. One of great feats of seamanship told in delightful manner. 67 illustrations. 294pp. 5⅜ x 8½. 20326-3 Pa. $5.95

ANARCHISM AND OTHER ESSAYS, Emma Goldman. Powerful, penetrating, prophetic essays on direct action, role of minorities, prison reform, puritan hypocrisy, violence, etc. 271pp. 5⅜ x 8½. 22484-8 Pa. $6.95

MYTHS OF THE HINDUS AND BUDDHISTS, Ananda K. Coomaraswamy and Sister Nivedita. Great stories of the epics; deeds of Krishna, Shiva, taken from puranas, Vedas, folk tales; etc. 32 illustrations. 400pp. 5⅜ x 8½. 21759-0 Pa. $10.95

BEYOND PSYCHOLOGY, Otto Rank. Fear of death, desire of immortality, nature of sexuality, social organization, creativity, according to Rankian system. 291pp. 5⅜ x 8½. 20485-5 Pa. $8.95

A THEOLOGICO-POLITICAL TREATISE, Benedict Spinoza. Also contains unfinished Political Treatise. Great classic on religious liberty, theory of government on common consent. R. Elwes translation. Total of 421pp. 5⅜ x 8½. 20249-6 Pa. $9.95

MY BONDAGE AND MY FREEDOM, Frederick Douglass. Born a slave, Douglass became outspoken force in antislavery movement. The best of Douglass' autobiographies. Graphic description of slave life. 464pp. 5⅜ x 8½. 22457-0 Pa. $8.95

FOLLOWING THE EQUATOR: A Journey Around the World, Mark Twain. Fascinating humorous account of 1897 voyage to Hawaii, Australia, India, New Zealand, etc. Ironic, bemused reports on peoples, customs, climate, flora and fauna, politics, much more. 197 illustrations. 720pp. 5⅜ x 8½. 26113-1 Pa. $15.95

THE PEOPLE CALLED SHAKERS, Edward D. Andrews. Definitive study of Shakers: origins, beliefs, practices, dances, social organization, furniture and crafts, etc. 33 illustrations. 351pp. 5⅜ x 8½. 21081-2 Pa. $8.95

THE MYTHS OF GREECE AND ROME, H. A. Guerber. A classic of mythology, generously illustrated, long prized for its simple, graphic, accurate retelling of the principal myths of Greece and Rome, and for its commentary on their origins and significance. With 64 illustrations by Michelangelo, Raphael, Titian, Rubens, Canova, Bernini and others. 480pp. 5⅜ x 8½. 27584-1 Pa. $9.95

PSYCHOLOGY OF MUSIC, Carl E. Seashore. Classic work discusses music as a medium from psychological viewpoint. Clear treatment of physical acoustics, auditory apparatus, sound perception, development of musical skills, nature of musical feeling, host of other topics. 88 figures. 408pp. 5⅜ x 8½. 21851-1 Pa. $10.95

THE PHILOSOPHY OF HISTORY, Georg W. Hegel. Great classic of Western thought develops concept that history is not chance but rational process, the evolution of freedom. 457pp. 5⅜ x 8½. 20112-0 Pa. $9.95

THE BOOK OF TEA, Kakuzo Okakura. Minor classic of the Orient: entertaining, charming explanation, interpretation of traditional Japanese culture in terms of tea ceremony. 94pp. 5⅜ x 8½. 20070-1 Pa. $3.95

LIFE IN ANCIENT EGYPT, Adolf Erman. Fullest, most thorough, detailed older account with much not in more recent books, domestic life, religion, magic, medicine, commerce, much more. Many illustrations reproduce tomb paintings, carvings, hieroglyphs, etc. 597pp. 5⅜ x 8½. 22632-8 Pa. $11.95

SUNDIALS, Their Theory and Construction, Albert Waugh. Far and away the best, most thorough coverage of ideas, mathematics concerned, types, construction, adjusting anywhere. Simple, nontechnical treatment allows even children to build several of these dials. Over 100 illustrations. 230pp. 5⅜ x 8½. 22947-5 Pa. $7.95

DYNAMICS OF FLUIDS IN POROUS MEDIA, Jacob Bear. For advanced students of ground water hydrology, soil mechanics and physics, drainage and irrigation engineering, and more. 335 illustrations. Exercises, with answers. 784pp. 6⅛ x 9¼. 65675-6 Pa. $19.95

SONGS OF EXPERIENCE: Facsimile Reproduction with 26 Plates in Full Color, William Blake. 26 full-color plates from a rare 1826 edition. Includes "The Tyger," "London," "Holy Thursday," and other poems. Printed text of poems. 48pp. 5¼ x 7. 24636-1 Pa. $4.95

OLD-TIME VIGNETTES IN FULL COLOR, Carol Belanger Grafton (ed.). Over 390 charming, often sentimental illustrations, selected from archives of Victorian graphics—pretty women posing, children playing, food, flowers, kittens and puppies, smiling cherubs, birds and butterflies, much more. All copyright-free. 48pp. 9¼ x 12¼. 27269-9 Pa. $7.95

PERSPECTIVE FOR ARTISTS, Rex Vicat Cole. Depth, perspective of sky and sea, shadows, much more, not usually covered. 391 diagrams, 81 reproductions of drawings and paintings. 279pp. 5⅜ x 8½. 22487-2 Pa. $7.95

DRAWING THE LIVING FIGURE, Joseph Sheppard. Innovative approach to artistic anatomy focuses on specifics of surface anatomy, rather than muscles and bones. Over 170 drawings of live models in front, back and side views, and in widely varying poses. Accompanying diagrams. 177 illustrations. Introduction. Index. 144pp. 8⅜ x11¼. 26723-7 Pa. $8.95

GOTHIC AND OLD ENGLISH ALPHABETS: 100 Complete Fonts, Dan X. Solo. Add power, elegance to posters, signs, other graphics with 100 stunning copyright-free alphabets: Blackstone, Dolbey, Germania, 97 more–including many lower-case, numerals, punctuation marks. 104pp. 8⅛ x 11. 24695-7 Pa. $8.95

HOW TO DO BEADWORK, Mary White. Fundamental book on craft from simple projects to five-bead chains and woven works. 106 illustrations. 142pp. 5⅜ x 8. 20697-1 Pa. $4.95

THE BOOK OF WOOD CARVING, Charles Marshall Sayers. Finest book for beginners discusses fundamentals and offers 34 designs. "Absolutely first rate . . . well thought out and well executed."–E. J. Tangerman. 118pp. 7¾ x 10⅝. 23654-4 Pa. $6.95

ILLUSTRATED CATALOG OF CIVIL WAR MILITARY GOODS: Union Army Weapons, Insignia, Uniform Accessories, and Other Equipment, Schuyler, Hartley, and Graham. Rare, profusely illustrated 1846 catalog includes Union Army uniform and dress regulations, arms and ammunition, coats, insignia, flags, swords, rifles, etc. 226 illustrations. 160pp. 9 x 12. 24939-5 Pa. $10.95

WOMEN'S FASHIONS OF THE EARLY 1900s: An Unabridged Republication of "New York Fashions, 1909," National Cloak & Suit Co. Rare catalog of mail-order fashions documents women's and children's clothing styles shortly after the turn of the century. Captions offer full descriptions, prices. Invaluable resource for fashion, costume historians. Approximately 725 illustrations. 128pp. 8⅜ x 11¼. 27276-1 Pa. $11.95

THE 1912 AND 1915 GUSTAV STICKLEY FURNITURE CATALOGS, Gustav Stickley. With over 200 detailed illustrations and descriptions, these two catalogs are essential reading and reference materials and identification guides for Stickley furniture. Captions cite materials, dimensions and prices. 112pp. 6½ x 9¼. 26676-1 Pa. $9.95

EARLY AMERICAN LOCOMOTIVES, John H. White, Jr. Finest locomotive engravings from early 19th century: historical (1804–74), main-line (after 1870), special, foreign, etc. 147 plates. 142pp. 11⅜ x 8¼. 22772-3 Pa. $10.95

THE TALL SHIPS OF TODAY IN PHOTOGRAPHS, Frank O. Braynard. Lavishly illustrated tribute to nearly 100 majestic contemporary sailing vessels: Amerigo Vespucci, Clearwater, Constitution, Eagle, Mayflower, Sea Cloud, Victory, many more. Authoritative captions provide statistics, background on each ship. 190 black-and-white photographs and illustrations. Introduction. 128pp. 8⅞ x 11¾. 27163-3 Pa. $13.95

EARLY NINETEENTH-CENTURY CRAFTS AND TRADES, Peter Stockham (ed.). Extremely rare 1807 volume describes to youngsters the crafts and trades of the day: brickmaker, weaver, dressmaker, bookbinder, ropemaker, saddler, many more. Quaint prose, charming illustrations for each craft. 20 black-and-white line illustrations. 192pp. 4⅝ x 6. 27293-1 Pa. $4.95

VICTORIAN FASHIONS AND COSTUMES FROM HARPER'S BAZAR, 1867–1898, Stella Blum (ed.). Day costumes, evening wear, sports clothes, shoes, hats, other accessories in over 1,000 detailed engravings. 320pp. 9⅜ x 12¼. 22990-4 Pa. $14.95

GUSTAV STICKLEY, THE CRAFTSMAN, Mary Ann Smith. Superb study surveys broad scope of Stickley's achievement, especially in architecture. Design philosophy, rise and fall of the Craftsman empire, descriptions and floor plans for many Craftsman houses, more. 86 black-and-white halftones. 31 line illustrations. Introduction 208pp. 6½ x 9¼. 27210-9 Pa. $9.95

THE LONG ISLAND RAIL ROAD IN EARLY PHOTOGRAPHS, Ron Ziel. Over 220 rare photos, informative text document origin (1844) and development of rail service on Long Island. Vintage views of early trains, locomotives, stations, passengers, crews, much more. Captions. 8⅞ x 11¾. 26301-0 Pa. $13.95

THE BOOK OF OLD SHIPS: From Egyptian Galleys to Clipper Ships, Henry B. Culver. Superb, authoritative history of sailing vessels, with 80 magnificent line illustrations. Galley, bark, caravel, longship, whaler, many more. Detailed, informative text on each vessel by noted naval historian. Introduction. 256pp. 5⅜ x 8½. 27332-6 Pa. $7.95

TEN BOOKS ON ARCHITECTURE, Vitruvius. The most important book ever written on architecture. Early Roman aesthetics, technology, classical orders, site selection, all other aspects. Morgan translation. 331pp. 5⅜ x 8½. 20645-9 Pa. $8.95

THE HUMAN FIGURE IN MOTION, Eadweard Muybridge. More than 4,500 stopped-action photos, in action series, showing undraped men, women, children jumping, lying down, throwing, sitting, wrestling, carrying, etc. 390pp. 7⅞ x 10⅝. 20204-6 Clothbd. $25.95

TREES OF THE EASTERN AND CENTRAL UNITED STATES AND CANADA, William M. Harlow. Best one-volume guide to 140 trees. Full descriptions, woodlore, range, etc. Over 600 illustrations. Handy size. 288pp. 4½ x 6⅜. 20395-6 Pa. $6.95

SONGS OF WESTERN BIRDS, Dr. Donald J. Borror. Complete song and call repertoire of 60 western species, including flycatchers, juncoes, cactus wrens, many more–includes fully illustrated booklet. Cassette and manual 99913-0 $8.95

GROWING AND USING HERBS AND SPICES, Milo Miloradovich. Versatile handbook provides all the information needed for cultivation and use of all the herbs and spices available in North America. 4 illustrations. Index. Glossary. 236pp. 5⅜ x 8½. 25058-X Pa. $6.95

BIG BOOK OF MAZES AND LABYRINTHS, Walter Shepherd. 50 mazes and labyrinths in all–classical, solid, ripple, and more–in one great volume. Perfect inexpensive puzzler for clever youngsters. Full solutions. 112pp. 8⅛ x 11. 22951-3 Pa. $4.95

PIANO TUNING, J. Cree Fischer. Clearest, best book for beginner, amateur. Simple repairs, raising dropped notes, tuning by easy method of flattened fifths. No previous skills needed. 4 illustrations. 201pp. 5⅜ x 8½. 23267-0 Pa. $6.95

A SOURCE BOOK IN THEATRICAL HISTORY, A. M. Nagler. Contemporary observers on acting, directing, make-up, costuming, stage props, machinery, scene design, from Ancient Greece to Chekhov. 611pp. 5⅜ x 8½. 20515-0 Pa. $12.95

THE COMPLETE NONSENSE OF EDWARD LEAR, Edward Lear. All nonsense limericks, zany alphabets, Owl and Pussycat, songs, nonsense botany, etc., illustrated by Lear. Total of 320pp. 5⅜ x 8½. (USO) 20167-8 Pa. $6.95

VICTORIAN PARLOUR POETRY: An Annotated Anthology, Michael R. Turner. 117 gems by Longfellow, Tennyson, Browning, many lesser-known poets. "The Village Blacksmith," "Curfew Must Not Ring Tonight," "Only a Baby Small," dozens more, often difficult to find elsewhere. Index of poets, titles, first lines. xxiii + 325pp. 5⅜ x 8¼. 27044-0 Pa. $8.95

DUBLINERS, James Joyce. Fifteen stories offer vivid, tightly focused observations of the lives of Dublin's poorer classes. At least one, "The Dead," is considered a masterpiece. Reprinted complete and unabridged from standard edition. 160pp. 5 3/16 x 8¼. 26870-5 Pa. $1.00

THE HAUNTED MONASTERY and THE CHINESE MAZE MURDERS, Robert van Gulik. Two full novels by van Gulik, set in 7th-century China, continue adventures of Judge Dee and his companions. An evil Taoist monastery, seemingly supernatural events; overgrown topiary maze hides strange crimes. 27 illustrations. 328pp. 5⅜ x 8½. 23502-5 Pa. $8.95

THE BOOK OF THE SACRED MAGIC OF ABRAMELIN THE MAGE, translated by S. MacGregor Mathers. Medieval manuscript of ceremonial magic. Basic document in Aleister Crowley, Golden Dawn groups. 268pp. 5⅜ x 8½. 23211-5 Pa. $8.95

NEW RUSSIAN-ENGLISH AND ENGLISH-RUSSIAN DICTIONARY, M. A. O'Brien. This is a remarkably handy Russian dictionary, containing a surprising amount of information, including over 70,000 entries. 366pp. 4½ x 6⅛. 20208-9 Pa. $9.95

HISTORIC HOMES OF THE AMERICAN PRESIDENTS, Second, Revised Edition, Irvin Haas. A traveler's guide to American Presidential homes, most open to the public, depicting and describing homes occupied by every American President from George Washington to George Bush. With visiting hours, admission charges, travel routes. 175 photographs. Index. 160pp. 8¼ x 11. 26751-2 Pa. $11.95

NEW YORK IN THE FORTIES, Andreas Feininger. 162 brilliant photographs by the well-known photographer, formerly with *Life* magazine. Commuters, shoppers, Times Square at night, much else from city at its peak. Captions by John von Hartz. 181pp. 9¼ x 10¾. 23585-8 Pa. $12.95

INDIAN SIGN LANGUAGE, William Tomkins. Over 525 signs developed by Sioux and other tribes. Written instructions and diagrams. Also 290 pictographs. 111pp. 6⅛ x 9¼. 22029-X Pa. $3.95

ANATOMY: A Complete Guide for Artists, Joseph Sheppard. A master of figure drawing shows artists how to render human anatomy convincingly. Over 460 illustrations. 224pp. 8⅜ x 11¼.   27279-6 Pa. $10.95

MEDIEVAL CALLIGRAPHY: Its History and Technique, Marc Drogin. Spirited history, comprehensive instruction manual covers 13 styles (ca. 4th century thru 15th). Excellent photographs; directions for duplicating medieval techniques with modern tools. 224pp. 8⅜ x 11¼.   26142-5 Pa. $12.95

DRIED FLOWERS: How to Prepare Them, Sarah Whitlock and Martha Rankin. Complete instructions on how to use silica gel, meal and borax, perlite aggregate, sand and borax, glycerine and water to create attractive permanent flower arrangements. 12 illustrations. 32pp. 5⅜ x 8½.   21802-3 Pa. $1.00

EASY-TO-MAKE BIRD FEEDERS FOR WOODWORKERS, Scott D. Campbell. Detailed, simple-to-use guide for designing, constructing, caring for and using feeders. Text, illustrations for 12 classic and contemporary designs. 96pp. 5⅜ x 8½.
25847-5 Pa. $2.95

SCOTTISH WONDER TALES FROM MYTH AND LEGEND, Donald A. Mackenzie. 16 lively tales tell of giants rumbling down mountainsides, of a magic wand that turns stone pillars into warriors, of gods and goddesses, evil hags, powerful forces and more. 240pp. 5⅜ x 8½.   29677-6 Pa. $6.95

THE HISTORY OF UNDERCLOTHES, C. Willett Cunnington and Phyllis Cunnington. Fascinating, well-documented survey covering six centuries of English undergarments, enhanced with over 100 illustrations: 12th-century laced-up bodice, footed long drawers (1795), 19th-century bustles, 19th-century corsets for men, Victorian "bust improvers," much more. 272pp. 5⅜ x 8¼.   27124-2 Pa. $9.95

ARTS AND CRAFTS FURNITURE: The Complete Brooks Catalog of 1912, ‸Brooks Manufacturing Co. Photos and detailed descriptions of more than 150 now very collectible furniture designs from the Arts and Crafts movement depict davenports, settees, buffets, desks, tables, chairs, bedsteads, dressers and more, all built of solid, quarter-sawed oak. Invaluable for students and enthusiasts of antiques, Americana and the decorative arts. 80pp. 6½ x 9¼.   27471-3 Pa. $8.95

HOW WE INVENTED THE AIRPLANE: An Illustrated History, Orville Wright. Fascinating firsthand account covers early experiments, construction of planes and motors, first flights, much more. Introduction and commentary by Fred C. Kelly. 76 photographs. 96pp. 8¼ x 11.   25662-6 Pa. $8.95

THE ARTS OF THE SAILOR: Knotting, Splicing and Ropework, Hervey Garrett Smith. Indispensable shipboard reference covers tools, basic knots and useful hitches; handsewing and canvas work, more. Over 100 illustrations. Delightful reading for sea lovers. 256pp. 5⅜ x 8½.   26440-8 Pa. $7.95

FRANK LLOYD WRIGHT'S FALLINGWATER: The House and Its History, Second, Revised Edition, Donald Hoffmann. A total revision—both in text and illustrations—of the standard document on Fallingwater, the boldest, most personal architectural statement of Wright's mature years, updated with valuable new material from the recently opened Frank Lloyd Wright Archives. "Fascinating"—*The New York Times.* 116 illustrations. 128pp. 9¼ x 10¾.   27430-6 Pa. $11.95

PHOTOGRAPHIC SKETCHBOOK OF THE CIVIL WAR, Alexander Gardner. 100 photos taken on field during the Civil War. Famous shots of Manassas Harper's Ferry, Lincoln, Richmond, slave pens, etc. 244pp. 10⅝ x 8¼. 22731-6 Pa. $9.95

FIVE ACRES AND INDEPENDENCE, Maurice G. Kains. Great back-to-the-land classic explains basics of self-sufficient farming. The one book to get. 95 illustrations. 397pp. 5⅜ x 8½. 20974-1 Pa. $7.95

SONGS OF EASTERN BIRDS, Dr. Donald J. Borror. Songs and calls of 60 species most common to eastern U.S.: warblers, woodpeckers, flycatchers, thrushes, larks, many more in high-quality recording. Cassette and manual 99912-2 $9.95

A MODERN HERBAL, Margaret Grieve. Much the fullest, most exact, most useful compilation of herbal material. Gigantic alphabetical encyclopedia, from aconite to zedoary, gives botanical information, medical properties, folklore, economic uses, much else. Indispensable to serious reader. 161 illustrations. 888pp. 6½ x 9¼. 2-vol. set. (USO) Vol. I: 22798-7 Pa. $9.95
Vol. II: 22799-5 Pa. $9.95

HIDDEN TREASURE MAZE BOOK, Dave Phillips. Solve 34 challenging mazes accompanied by heroic tales of adventure. Evil dragons, people-eating plants, blood-thirsty giants, many more dangerous adversaries lurk at every twist and turn. 34 mazes, stories, solutions. 48pp. 8¼ x 11. 24566-7 Pa. $2.95

LETTERS OF W. A. MOZART, Wolfgang A. Mozart. Remarkable letters show bawdy wit, humor, imagination, musical insights, contemporary musical world; includes some letters from Leopold Mozart. 276pp. 5⅜ x 8½. 22859-2 Pa. $7.95

BASIC PRINCIPLES OF CLASSICAL BALLET, Agrippina Vaganova. Great Russian theoretician, teacher explains methods for teaching classical ballet. 118 illustrations. 175pp. 5⅜ x 8½. 22036-2 Pa. $5.95

THE JUMPING FROG, Mark Twain. Revenge edition. The original story of The Celebrated Jumping Frog of Calaveras County, a hapless French translation, and Twain's hilarious "retranslation" from the French. 12 illustrations. 66pp. 5⅜ x 8½. 22686-7 Pa. $3.95

BEST REMEMBERED POEMS, Martin Gardner (ed.). The 126 poems in this superb collection of 19th- and 20th-century British and American verse range from Shelley's "To a Skylark" to the impassioned "Renascence" of Edna St. Vincent Millay and to Edward Lear's whimsical "The Owl and the Pussycat." 224pp. 5⅜ x 8½. 27165-X Pa. $4.95

COMPLETE SONNETS, William Shakespeare. Over 150 exquisite poems deal with love, friendship, the tyranny of time, beauty's evanescence, death and other themes in language of remarkable power, precision and beauty. Glossary of archaic terms. 80pp. 5 3/16 x 8¼. 26686-9 Pa. $1.00

BODIES IN A BOOKSHOP, R. T. Campbell. Challenging mystery of blackmail and murder with ingenious plot and superbly drawn characters. In the best tradition of British suspense fiction. 192pp. 5⅜ x 8½. 24720-1 Pa. $6.95

THE WIT AND HUMOR OF OSCAR WILDE, Alvin Redman (ed.). More than 1,000 ripostes, paradoxes, wisecracks: Work is the curse of the drinking classes; I can resist everything except temptation; etc. 258pp. 5⅜ x 8½. 20602-5 Pa. $5.95

SHAKESPEARE LEXICON AND QUOTATION DICTIONARY, Alexander Schmidt. Full definitions, locations, shades of meaning in every word in plays and poems. More than 50,000 exact quotations. 1,485pp. 6½ x 9¼. 2-vol. set.
Vol. 1: 22726-X Pa. $16.95
Vol. 2: 22727-8 Pa. $16.95

SELECTED POEMS, Emily Dickinson. Over 100 best-known, best-loved poems by one of America's foremost poets, reprinted from authoritative early editions. No comparable edition at this price. Index of first lines. 64pp. 5³⁄₁₆ x 8¼.
26466-1 Pa. $1.00

CELEBRATED CASES OF JUDGE DEE (DEE GOONG AN), translated by Robert van Gulik. Authentic 18th-century Chinese detective novel; Dee and associates solve three interlocked cases. Led to van Gulik's own stories with same characters. Extensive introduction. 9 illustrations. 237pp. 5⅜ x 8½. 23337-5 Pa. $6.95

THE MALLEUS MALEFICARUM OF KRAMER AND SPRENGER, translated by Montague Summers. Full text of most important witchhunter's "bible," used by both Catholics and Protestants. 278pp. 6⅝ x 10. 22802-9 Pa. $12.95

SPANISH STORIES/CUENTOS ESPAÑOLES: A Dual-Language Book, Angel Flores (ed.). Unique format offers 13 great stories in Spanish by Cervantes, Borges, others. Faithful English translations on facing pages. 352pp. 5⅜ x 8½.
25399-6 Pa. $8.95

THE CHICAGO WORLD'S FAIR OF 1893: A Photographic Record, Stanley Appelbaum (ed.). 128 rare photos show 200 buildings, Beaux-Arts architecture, Midway, original Ferris Wheel, Edison's kinetoscope, more. Architectural emphasis; full text. 116pp. 8¼ x 11. 23990-X Pa. $9.95

OLD QUEENS, N.Y., IN EARLY PHOTOGRAPHS, Vincent F. Seyfried and William Asadorian. Over 160 rare photographs of Maspeth, Jamaica, Jackson Heights, and other areas. Vintage views of DeWitt Clinton mansion, 1939 World's Fair and more. Captions. 192pp. 8⅞ x 11. 26358-4 Pa. $12.95

CAPTURED BY THE INDIANS: 15 Firsthand Accounts, 1750-1870, Frederick Drimmer. Astounding true historical accounts of grisly torture, bloody conflicts, relentless pursuits, miraculous escapes and more, by people who lived to tell the tale. 384pp. 5⅜ x 8½. 24901-8 Pa. $8.95

THE WORLD'S GREAT SPEECHES, Lewis Copeland and Lawrence W. Lamm (eds.). Vast collection of 278 speeches of Greeks to 1970. Powerful and effective models; unique look at history. 842pp. 5⅜ x 8½. 20468-5 Pa. $14.95

THE BOOK OF THE SWORD, Sir Richard F. Burton. Great Victorian scholar/adventurer's eloquent, erudite history of the "queen of weapons"—from prehistory to early Roman Empire. Evolution and development of early swords, variations (sabre, broadsword, cutlass, scimitar, etc.), much more. 336pp. 6⅛ x 9¼.
25434-8 Pa. $9.95

AUTOBIOGRAPHY: The Story of My Experiments with Truth, Mohandas K. Gandhi. Boyhood, legal studies, purification, the growth of the Satyagraha (nonviolent protest) movement. Critical, inspiring work of the man responsible for the freedom of India. 480pp. 5⅜ x 8½. (USO) 24593-4 Pa. $8.95

CELTIC MYTHS AND LEGENDS, T. W. Rolleston. Masterful retelling of Irish and Welsh stories and tales. Cuchulain, King Arthur, Deirdre, the Grail, many more. First paperback edition. 58 full-page illustrations. 512pp. 5⅜ x 8½. 26507-2 Pa. $9.95

THE PRINCIPLES OF PSYCHOLOGY, William James. Famous long course complete, unabridged. Stream of thought, time perception, memory, experimental methods; great work decades ahead of its time. 94 figures. 1,391pp. 5⅜ x 8½. 2-vol. set.
Vol. I: 20381-6 Pa. $12.95
Vol. II: 20382-4 Pa. $12.95

THE WORLD AS WILL AND REPRESENTATION, Arthur Schopenhauer. Definitive English translation of Schopenhauer's life work, correcting more than 1,000 errors, omissions in earlier translations. Translated by E. F. J. Payne. Total of 1,269pp. 5⅜ x 8½. 2-vol. set. Vol. 1: 21761-2 Pa. $11.95
Vol. 2: 21762-0 Pa. $12.95

MAGIC AND MYSTERY IN TIBET, Madame Alexandra David-Neel. Experiences among lamas, magicians, sages, sorcerers, Bonpa wizards. A true psychic discovery. 32 illustrations. 321pp. 5⅜ x 8½. (USO) 22682-4 Pa. $8.95

THE EGYPTIAN BOOK OF THE DEAD, E. A. Wallis Budge. Complete reproduction of Ani's papyrus, finest ever found. Full hieroglyphic text, interlinear transliteration, word-for-word translation, smooth translation. 533pp. 6½ x 9¼.
21866-X Pa. $10.95

MATHEMATICS FOR THE NONMATHEMATICIAN, Morris Kline. Detailed, college-level treatment of mathematics in cultural and historical context, with numerous exercises. Recommended Reading Lists. Tables. Numerous figures. 641pp. 5⅜ x 8½.
24823-2 Pa. $11.95

THEORY OF WING SECTIONS: Including a Summary of Airfoil Data, Ira H. Abbott and A. E. von Doenhoff. Concise compilation of subsonic aerodynamic characteristics of NACA wing sections, plus description of theory. 350pp. of tables. 693pp. 5⅜ x 8½. 60586-8 Pa. $14.95

THE RIME OF THE ANCIENT MARINER, Gustave Doré, S. T. Coleridge. Doré's finest work; 34 plates capture moods, subtleties of poem. Flawless full-size reproductions printed on facing pages with authoritative text of poem. "Beautiful. Simply beautiful."—*Publisher's Weekly*. 77pp. 9¼ x 12. 22305-1 Pa. $6.95

NORTH AMERICAN INDIAN DESIGNS FOR ARTISTS AND CRAFTSPEOPLE, Eva Wilson. Over 360 authentic copyright-free designs adapted from Navajo blankets, Hopi pottery, Sioux buffalo hides, more. Geometrics, symbolic figures, plant and animal motifs, etc. 128pp. 8⅜ x 11. (EUK) 25341-4 Pa. $8.95

SCULPTURE: Principles and Practice, Louis Slobodkin. Step-by-step approach to clay, plaster, metals, stone; classical and modern. 253 drawings, photos. 255pp. 8⅛ x 11.
22960-2 Pa. $11.95

CATALOG OF DOVER BOOKS

THE INFLUENCE OF SEA POWER UPON HISTORY, 1660–1783, A. T. Mahan. Influential classic of naval history and tactics still used as text in war colleges. First paperback edition. 4 maps. 24 battle plans. 640pp. 5⅜ x 8½. 25509-3 Pa. $12.95

THE STORY OF THE TITANIC AS TOLD BY ITS SURVIVORS, Jack Winocour (ed.). What it was really like. Panic, despair, shocking inefficiency, and a little heroism. More thrilling than any fictional account. 26 illustrations. 320pp. 5⅜ x 8½. 20610-6 Pa. $8.95

FAIRY AND FOLK TALES OF THE IRISH PEASANTRY, William Butler Yeats (ed.). Treasury of 64 tales from the twilight world of Celtic myth and legend: "The Soul Cages," "The Kildare Pooka," "King O'Toole and his Goose," many more. Introduction and Notes by W. B. Yeats. 352pp. 5⅜ x 8½. 26941-8 Pa. $8.95

BUDDHIST MAHAYANA TEXTS, E. B. Cowell and Others (eds.). Superb, accurate translations of basic documents in Mahayana Buddhism, highly important in history of religions. The Buddha-karita of Asvaghosha, Larger Sukhavativyuha, more. 448pp. 5⅜ x 8½. 25552-2 Pa. $12.95

ONE TWO THREE . . . INFINITY: Facts and Speculations of Science, George Gamow. Great physicist's fascinating, readable overview of contemporary science: number theory, relativity, fourth dimension, entropy, genes, atomic structure, much more. 128 illustrations. Index. 352pp. 5⅜ x 8½. 25664-2 Pa. $8.95

ENGINEERING IN HISTORY, Richard Shelton Kirby, et al. Broad, nontechnical survey of history's major technological advances: birth of Greek science, industrial revolution, electricity and applied science, 20th-century automation, much more. 181 illustrations. ". . . excellent . . ."–Isis. Bibliography. vii + 530pp. 5⅜ x 8¼. 26412-2 Pa. $14.95

DALÍ ON MODERN ART: The Cuckolds of Antiquated Modern Art, Salvador Dalí. Influential painter skewers modern art and its practitioners. Outrageous evaluations of Picasso, Cézanne, Turner, more. 15 renderings of paintings discussed. 44 calligraphic decorations by Dalí. 96pp. 5⅜ x 8½. (USO) 29220-7 Pa. $4.95

ANTIQUE PLAYING CARDS: A Pictorial History, Henry René D'Allemagne. Over 900 elaborate, decorative images from rare playing cards (14th–20th centuries): Bacchus, death, dancing dogs, hunting scenes, royal coats of arms, players cheating, much more. 96pp. 9¼ x 12¼. 29265-7 Pa. $11.95

MAKING FURNITURE MASTERPIECES: 30 Projects with Measured Drawings, Franklin H. Gottshall. Step-by-step instructions, illustrations for constructing handsome, useful pieces, among them a Sheraton desk, Chippendale chair, Spanish desk, Queen Anne table and a William and Mary dressing mirror. 224pp. 8⅛ x 11¼. 29338-6 Pa. $13.95

THE FOSSIL BOOK: A Record of Prehistoric Life, Patricia V. Rich et al. Profusely illustrated definitive guide covers everything from single-celled organisms and dinosaurs to birds and mammals and the interplay between climate and man. Over 1,500 illustrations. 760pp. 7½ x 10⅛. 29371-8 Pa. $29.95

Prices subject to change without notice.
Available at your book dealer or write for free catalog to Dept. GI, Dover Publications, Inc., 31 East 2nd St., Mineola, N.Y. 11501. Dover publishes more than 500 books each year on science, elementary and advanced mathematics, biology, music, art, literary history, social sciences and other areas.